THE ESSENTIAL BEGINNERS GUIDE TO BUDDHISM

A Guide to the Philosophy; Reveal the Path to
Transform Your Life; Get Rid of Stress and Anxiety;
Achieve Understanding, Compassion, Wisdom,
Calm and Peace

Rohini Heendeniya

Published by Phoenix ePublishing
www.phoenixepublishing.com

Cover Design by Angela Alaya

First Edition: July 2023

Contents

INTRODUCTION

You may think of Buddhism as a religion - in fact, it is the fourth largest faith-based belief system in the world. Perhaps you associate it with words like 'Enlightenment', 'Nirvana', or 'Karma'. You may have an idea that it has something to do with meditation and mindfulness, but perhaps you're unsure of how it all fits together. These concepts have been around for over 2,500 years, far outdating many other philosophies and belief systems, and they have the potential to transform your life.

This book is not intended to be a dry distillation of canonical facts about the theories and teachings of Buddhism and its practices. There are many resources in innumerable authoritative treatises and books, as well as the internet, dissecting, discussing, and developing the meanings and practices within Buddhist philosophy. If you would like to learn more about the breadth and depth of Buddhist philosophy, then I encourage you to seek these out.

Instead, here you will find a straightforward introduction to the original teachings of the Lord Buddha and a methodical guide on how to integrate these wonderful lessons into your life. Numerous exercises and strategic approaches await you, facilitating deep contemplation, practice, and skillful integration of these profound teachings. These transformative practices empower and illuminate your journey toward unlocking the boundless reservoir of abundance residing within your being. Moving you from perceiving life through muted sepia tones, to experiencing it as a vibrant tapestry of colors.

As Buddhism transcends conventional dogma, it presents itself as a philosophical framework – a sacred guide to unveiling the path to enlightenment. Unlike the prescriptive nature of Judeo-Christian traditions, the principles and concepts inherent in Buddhism do not impose themselves as rigid commandments. They are more like guidelines. Similarly, there is no distinct 'God' who is the judge or arbiter of ethical action. You choose your thoughts and actions. As in the Five Precepts, the purpose is to go beyond notions of right and wrong. It doesn't impose or require you to follow the teachings. That is not possible; the desire to follow them must be an internal and foundational desire on your part.

"Life is suffering." This stark declaration, attributed to Buddha, might seem shocking or even depressing at first glance. Yet, it is the foundation upon which Buddhism is built. It's the first of the Four Noble Truths, the cornerstone of Buddhist philosophy. These words aren't intended to induce despair but rather to awaken us to a fundamental reality of existence, prompting us to seek a deeper understanding and, ultimately, liberation from suffering. This is where our journey into Buddhism begins.

There's an old Buddhist parable about a man who was shot with a poisoned arrow. Rather than allowing the arrow to be removed, the man insisted on knowing who shot the arrow, what kind of wood it was made of, and what type of bird the feathers on it came from. While these questions were interesting, they weren't particularly helpful to his current predicament. His focus on the wrong details, on trivia rather than the matter at hand, ultimately led to his demise.

You might be living a life filled with seemingly endless obligations, deadlines, and stressors. The constant hustle and bustle, the never-ending to-do lists, and the incessant ping of notifications; they can all create a constant hum of anxiety and stress in your life. In this whirlwind of modern living, you might feel like a hamster on a wheel, continuously running but never truly moving forward. This can lead to a sense of frustration, dissatisfaction, and even despair.

I know because I've been there too. There was a time I found myself entangled in the ceaseless grind of life, feeling perpetually overwhelmed and often unfulfilled. It was at this juncture that I sought solace in the teachings of Buddhism, a philosophy (or religion, depending on one's perspective) that my family has practiced for generations.

Perhaps your days are filled with back-to-back meetings, endless emails, and countless other tasks that leave you feeling overwhelmed and drained. You may find yourself rushing from one task to the next, with little time to pause and breathe, let alone enjoy the simple pleasures of life. The pressure to keep up with this relentless pace can lead to stress, anxiety, and even depression.

Or maybe your struggle is more subtle. Perhaps you feel a sense of dissatisfaction or emptiness, even though you've achieved many of the things society tells us we should strive for - a successful career, a beautiful home, a loving family. Despite these accomplishments, you feel like something is missing. You yearn for a deeper sense of fulfilment, a sense of peace and contentment that doesn't depend on external circumstances.

Now, let's take a step back and look at the broader picture. We live in a society that constantly bombards us with messages telling us we need to do more, achieve more, be more. We are conditioned to believe that happiness comes from external achievements and possessions. But the truth is, these things can only provide temporary satisfaction. They cannot fill the inner void or bring lasting peace and happiness. This is one of the key insights of Buddhism.

Think about it. Have you ever achieved a long-desired goal, only to find that the happiness it brought was fleeting? Have you ever purchased something you really wanted, only to lose interest in it after a while? These experiences are common because they reflect the impermanent nature of external sources of happiness. They cannot satisfy our deeper longing for peace and fulfillment.

Buddhism offers a different perspective. It teaches us that true peace and happiness come from within, not from external circumstances. It offers a path to inner peace through mindfulness, meditation, and the cultivation of virtues like compassion, kindness, and wisdom.

"There is no path to happiness: happiness is the path." This quote from the Buddha serves as a reminder that the journey towards peace and fulfillment is not somewhere far off in the distance, but rather, it's right here in the present moment. As we embark on this exploration of the fundamental principles and concepts of Buddhism, it's important to remember that the benefits of these teachings are not reserved for some distant future. They can be experienced here and now, in your own life, in your own unique way.

One of the key benefits you'll gain from this exploration is a deeper understanding of yourself and your place in the world. Buddhism teaches us that we are not separate, isolated beings, but rather, we are interconnected with all of life. This realization can bring about a profound shift in perspective, helping you to see beyond the illusion of separation and recognize the interconnected nature of reality.

This understanding can have practical implications in your daily life. For instance, it can help you cultivate a sense of compassion and empathy, not just for others, but also for yourself. When you understand that your suffering is not separate from the suffering of others, you can begin to extend the same kindness and compassion to yourself that you offer to others. You can learn to treat yourself with the same care and respect that you extend to those around you, and in doing so, you can begin to heal from the inside out.

Another benefit is the cultivation of mindfulness and presence. In our busy, fast-paced world, it's easy to get caught up in the whirlwind of thoughts, worries, and distractions. We often find ourselves living in the past or the future, missing out on the richness of the present moment. Through the practice of mindfulness, you can learn to bring your attention back to the present moment, to fully engage with whatever you're doing, whether it's eating a meal, walking in nature, or having a conversation with a loved one. This can bring a sense of calm and clarity, helping you navigate the ups and downs of life with more grace and ease.

You'll also learn how to integrate these teachings into your everyday life. Buddhism is not about retreating from the world, but rather, it's about fully engaging with it, with mindfulness, compassion, and wisdom. Whether you're at work, at home, or in your community, you can apply these principles to enhance your relationships, improve your well-being, and contribute to a more compassionate and peaceful world.

For example, consider a typical day at work. You may have to deal with challenging situations, colleagues, demanding tasks, and tight deadlines. By applying the principles of mindfulness and compassion, you can learn to navigate these challenges with more ease and resilience. You can learn to respond rather than react, to listen deeply rather than react defensively, and to bring a sense of calm and clarity to even the most stressful situations.

Finally, there's the potential for personal transformation. Through the teachings and practices of Buddhism, you can learn to let go of unhelpful habits and patterns, cultivate positive qualities, and tap into your innate potential for wisdom and compassion. This can lead to a profound transformation, not just in your own life, but also in the lives of those around you.

"When we know ourselves, we are wise. When we serve others, we are healthy. When we unite with nature, we are holy." I stumbled upon this saying, attributed to the ancient Chinese philosopher Lao Tzu, during my early exploration of spirituality. It struck a chord in me and has guided my journey ever since. Now, let's take this journey together, you and I. Let's see what we can discover, learn, and integrate into our lives.

First and foremost, you will get to know the basic philosophies and concepts of Buddhism. You'll learn about the Four Noble Truths, which are the heart of Buddhism. These truths touch on the nature of suffering, its origin, its cessation, and the path leading to its cessation. You'll also explore the Eightfold Path, a practical guideline to ethical and mental development with the goal of freeing us from attachments and delusions.

You might have heard the term 'Nirvana' tossed around in popular culture, possibly without a clear understanding of what it really means. In this journey, we'll demystify Nirvana, exploring its meaning as the ultimate goal of Buddhist practice, a state of liberation and freedom from suffering. We'll also delve into the concept of 'Karma', often oversimplified as a system of cosmic justice. You'll learn that it is, in fact, a complex principle of cause and effect that governs our lives.

You'll discover the Three Universal Truths of Buddhism: impermanence, suffering, and the absence of self-nature. These might sound a bit abstract at first, but I assure you, understanding these principles can offer powerful insights into our own lives and the world around us.

Take, for instance, the principle of impermanence. It teaches us that everything changes and nothing remains constant. Understanding this can help us navigate life's ups and downs with grace and resilience. It can help us let go of our attachment to things, people, or situations, and instead appreciate them while they last. This understanding can bring a profound shift in our perspective, making us more resilient in the face of change.

Meditation and mindfulness, too, are integral parts of Buddhism that you'll learn to appreciate and practice. They are not just buzzwords, but deeply transformative practices that have been scientifically proven to benefit mental health. You'll understand how these practices can help manage stress, anxiety, depression, and other mental health conditions.

"Experience is the greatest teacher," so the saying goes. It's a simple truth, yet it carries enormous weight, especially when we talk about the journey of understanding and embracing a philosophy as profound as Buddhism. The insights that we gather along the way, the lessons we learn, and the transformations we undergo make us not just students, but also potential guides for others embarking on the same path. I want to share my journey with you, to help you navigate your own.

I was born into a Sri Lankan family where Buddhism was not just a belief system, but a way of life, a lens through which people viewed and engaged with their community and the world. However, moving and growing up in the UK from the early 1960s, my direct link to the practice of Buddhism was cut off. It was only later as an adult, while faced with a multitude of challenges, probably not dissimilar from that of most people, I made a conscious decision to change my life. I found ways to live a more conscious, fulfilling, and spiritual life, which offered me the unique opportunity to explore Buddhism and to see how its principles resonate and intersect with other philosophies and religions. It was an enriching experience that deepened my appreciation for Buddhism and its universal relevance.

My professional life has also played a significant part in my journey. I've worked in various industries, from transportation to property, in senior management roles. These experiences gave me first-hand exposure to the stress, pressure, and lack of fulfillment that many of us experience in our work lives. I saw how these negative experiences can seep into our personal lives, affecting our mental and physical health, our relationships, and our overall quality of life.

This realization led me to make a significant career shift. I decided to pursue my passion for healing and developing my own spirituality, training in a number of therapeutic practices, including Past Life Regression Therapy, energy meridian therapies such as Emotional Freedom Technique (EFT), and massage therapies including Tibetan Acupressure Massage, a technique based on ayurveda. These therapies, like Buddhism, are centered on the belief in our inherent potential for healing and transformation.

Throughout my journey, I've continued to learn, explore, and delve deeper into Buddhism and energetic healing practices. Through my first-hand experiences, I've seen how integrating Buddhist philosophical principles with the regular practice of mindfulness and meditation can bring about profound changes in one's mental, emotional, and physical well-being.

My journey, like yours, is ongoing. I continue to learn, grow, and transform. I want to share with you the wisdom I've gathered, the practices I've found helpful, and the insights I've gained. I want to help you navigate your own path, to live a more mindful, kind, and compassionate life.

Chapter One

AN OVERVIEW OF BUDDHISM

"Just as the great ocean has one taste, the taste of salt, so also this Dharma and Discipline has one taste, the taste of liberation" - Buddha

Definition and History of Buddhism

Buddhism, at its core, is not a religion, but a philosophical way of life. It's a journey of self-discovery, self-awakening, and self-transcendence. It was founded around the 5th century BCE by Prince Siddhartha Gautama, who later became known as the Buddha, or "the awakened one", Born into the royal Shakya clan in what is now Nepal, Siddhartha enjoyed a life of luxury and privilege. His father, the king, had been told by a seer that Siddhartha would either become a great king or a holy man. Fearing his son would abandon the throne, the king shielded him from the harsh realities of life, hoping to steer him towards a life of royal duty.

However, the protective bubble burst when Siddhartha, in his late 20s, ventured outside the palace walls. He was confronted with the harsh realities of life: illness, old age, and death. These were the truths hidden from him, and their revelation was a profound shock. He also encountered a serene ascetic, embodying a peace and fulfillment Siddhartha had never seen in his palace life. These experiences, often referred to as the "Four Sights," catalyzed Siddhartha's quest for understanding.

Siddhartha left his palace, his wife, and his newborn son to become a wandering ascetic. He sought wisdom from renowned spiritual teachers of his time, mastered their teachings, and even outdid them in their practices. But despite his severe austerities, the answers eluded him. He was seeking a path away from the suffering he had witnessed, but extreme asceticism only brought him physical pain and no closer to understanding.

Then one day, weakened and near death, Siddhartha accepted a bowl of rice milk from a village girl. In that moment, he realized the futility of his extreme practices. He decided to pursue a "Middle Way", a path of balance rather than extremism. He sat under a Bodhi tree and vowed not to rise until he had found the truth. After a long night of deep meditation, as the morning star rose, Siddhartha became the Buddha, the "awakened one". He had found the truth of existence and the path to liberation from suffering.

The Buddha was indeed a human being, not a deity or a saint. He did not claim divinity nor demand worship. Instead, he embodied the potential for transformation inherent in all of us. His teachings, known as Dhamma or Dharma, provide a detailed path that anyone can follow, a repertoire of methods that can lead to liberation.

This path is not about blind faith or unquestioning obedience, but about exploration and personal experience. The Buddha encouraged his followers to *"come and see"* the truth for themselves, and not simply to believe because he said so. His teachings are not mere philosophical ideas, but practical instructions for leading a life that brings wisdom, compassion, and inner peace.

During his first sermon at the deer park in Varanasi, the Buddha presented his discoveries as the Four Noble Truths and the Eightfold Path. This was his Middle Way, a path of moral living, meditation, and wisdom. It is a path that leads away from suffering and towards enlightenment, the ultimate liberation.

9

However, the wisdom imparted by the Buddha extends beyond personal transformation. They are also about how we interact with the world around us. The Buddha's teachings emphasize interdependence, underscoring the interconnectedness of all beings within the intricate fabric of existence. Our actions, thoughts, and words have ripple effects on others and the world at large. As we walk this path, we don't just transform ourselves; we also contribute to the transformation of the world.

Let me share a checklist that can guide you in your journey:

Learn: Start with the basic teachings of Buddhism, such as the Four Noble Truths and the Eightfold Path.

Meditate: Practice mindfulness and meditation regularly.

Apply: Incorporate Buddhist principles into your daily life.

Reflect: Contemplate the teachings and your experiences.

Connect: Join a community of practitioners for support and shared learning.

Remember, the path of Buddhism is not about reaching a destination, but about the journey itself. It's about continual growth, understanding, and transformation. As the Buddha taught, *"It is better to travel well than to arrive."*

Basic Beliefs and Philosophy of Buddhism

"All that we are is the result of what we have thought." These are profound words uttered by the Buddha that encapsulate the essence of Buddhist philosophy.

Buddhism, at its most fundamental level, is not a belief system that requires faith in a divine being. Rather, it is a pragmatic philosophy that encourages us to look within ourselves for wisdom and clarity. It encourages us to understand the nature of our minds and the reality of our existence.

The essence of Buddhist philosophy can be distilled into a handful of fundamental concepts.

First is the concept of Impermanence or *Anicca*. This is the understanding that all things are in a constant state of change. Nothing remains the same, not our bodies, not our thoughts, not even our emotions. Realizing this helps us to let go of attachments, and to appreciate each moment as it is, knowing it will not last.

The second is the concept of Unsatisfactoriness or *Dukkha*. *Dukkha* is often translated as suffering, but it also refers to the unsatisfactory nature of existence. It is the dissatisfaction we feel when we cling to impermanent things and experiences. The Buddha taught that *Dukkha* arises from our desires and aversions, from our craving and clinging.

The third concept is Non-Self or *Anatta*. This is the understanding that there is no permanent, unchanging self. Our sense of self is a construct of our minds, made up of constantly changing physical and mental processes. Recognizing this can free us from self-centered thoughts and behaviors, leading to greater compassion and understanding for others.

Understanding these three characteristics of existence—Impermanence, Unsatisfactoriness, and Non-Self—is crucial in Buddhist philosophy. They are interrelated and reinforce each other, providing a clear lens through which to view our lives and experiences.

The central teachings of the Buddha, the Four Noble Truths, and the Eightfold Path, provide practical guidance on how to navigate the realities of Impermanence, *Dukkha*, and *Anatta*. The Four Noble Truths diagnose the problem (*Dukkha*), identify the cause (craving and ignorance), declare that there is a solution (Nirvana or cessation of *Dukkha*), and prescribe a method (the Eightfold Path) for achieving it. The Eightfold Path is a comprehensive program for ethical living, mental discipline, and wisdom.

Remember, the beauty of Buddhist philosophy lies not in abstract intellectual understanding, but in putting the teachings into practice. It's not about accumulating knowledge, but about transforming our lives through wisdom and compassion.

How Buddhism Differs from Other Religions

"Buddhism has the characteristics of what would be expected in a cosmic religion for the future: It transcends a personal God, avoids dogmas and theology; it covers both the natural and spiritual; and it is based on a religious sense aspiring from the experience of all things, natural and spiritual, as a meaningful unity." These words from Albert Einstein, one of the greatest minds of the 20th century, offer a unique perspective on how Buddhism diverges from other religions.

Most faiths and religions center around a belief in a single God or a group of deities. These religions often propose a set of doctrines, rituals, and moral codes that followers are expected to adhere to. However, Buddhism takes a different path.

The first point of distinction is the absence of a personal creator god in Buddhism. While most religions position a god or gods as central figures, Buddhism does not. The Buddha was a man who achieved enlightenment, not a divine being. He taught that each individual has the capacity for awakening, emphasizing personal responsibility and self-realization rather than divine intervention.

Buddhism also places less emphasis on faith and more on practice. Other religions may demand unquestioning faith in a divine being or religious texts. But in Buddhism, the emphasis is on following the Noble Eightfold Path and cultivating wisdom through personal experience. The Buddha himself encouraged his followers to *"be a lamp unto yourself"* and to seek truth through personal experience rather than blind faith.

Buddhism's moral teachings, while similar to the ethical codes found in many religions, are presented not as divine commandments but as practical guidelines for leading a compassionate and fulfilling life. The Five Precepts of Buddhism - not to take life, not to take what is not given, not to engage in sexual misconduct, not to lie, and not to use intoxicants - are not seen as absolute commandments, but as guidelines that lead to personal and communal well-being.

Moreover, Buddhism recognizes the interdependent nature

of all existence, often captured in the concept of *Pratityasamutpada*, or Dependent Origination. This understanding of interconnectedness encourages a sense of universal responsibility and compassion that transcends the boundaries of self, community, or even species. This holistic perspective can provide a profound shift in how we relate to the world.

Let's consider a real-life example. Imagine you're stuck in a traffic jam, late for an important meeting. The stress and frustration are building up. In this situation, a Buddhist approach would be to practice mindfulness, observing your emotions without judgment. Then, cultivating compassion and understanding for the other drivers who are also stuck and probably feeling the same frustration. This shift in perspective can transform a stressful situation into an opportunity for personal growth and understanding.

"In the end, only three things matter: how much you loved, how gently you lived, and how gracefully you let go of things not meant for you." - Buddhist Proverb

Buddhism also differs in its view of the afterlife. While many religions have a concept of heaven and hell, Buddhism speaks of rebirth and the cycle of life, death, and rebirth, known as samsara. The ultimate goal is to achieve enlightenment and liberation from this cycle.

In short, Buddhism differs from other religions in its non-theistic foundation, emphasis on personal experience and practice over blind faith, ethical guidelines framed as practical advice rather than commandments, and the concept of interconnectedness.

However, it's essential to remember that these differences don't necessarily imply superiority or inferiority. Each religious tradition has its unique strengths and appeals to different individuals based on their personal experiences, values, and spiritual inclinations. As you continue your exploration of Buddhism, I invite you to approach it not as a replacement for other faiths, but as a path that offers unique insights into the nature of life, suffering, and the potential for liberation.

Chapter Two

THE FOUR NOBLE TRUTHS

"Everything changes, nothing remains without change." - Buddha

In a world that is constantly changing, there exist certain truths, steadfast and unwavering. These truths, recognized and taught by the Buddha, are known as the Four Noble Truths. They are not dependent on the presence of a Buddha in the world; they exist universally, regardless of time and space.

The Four Noble Truths:

- Suffering exists (Dukkha).

- Suffering has a cause (Samudaya).

- Suffering can cease (Nirodha).

- There is a path leading to the cessation of suffering (Magga).

These truths are not to be taken as pessimistic or negative; rather, they provide a realistic perspective of life as it is. The Buddha did not deny the existence of pleasure and happiness. Instead, he recognized these experiences as fleeting. True happiness, according to the Buddha, lies in understanding and transcending these transient experiences of life.

They provide a framework for understanding the challenges we face in our lives - whether it's stress at work, relationship problems, or health issues. By understanding the nature of suffering and its cause, we can work towards its cessation.

This quote beautifully encapsulates the essence of the Four Noble Truths. It reminds us of the inevitability of aging, sickness, and death - the ultimate forms of suffering. It also points towards the path to the cessation of suffering: living gently, loving deeply, and letting go gracefully.

The Truth of Dukkha (Suffering)

"The only way out of suffering is through it." This quote isn't from some ancient Buddhist text; it's from Carl Jung, one of the forefathers of modern psychology. Yet, it encapsulates an essential truth about Buddhism's first Noble Truth: The truth of *Dukkha*, or suffering.

Dukkha is often translated as suffering, but it encompasses much more. It represents the unsatisfactoriness, discontent, and general unease that pervades our lives. Life, in its impermanent nature, is filled with moments of joy, pain, love, and loss. But beneath the surface, there resides an ever-present undercurrent of dissatisfaction, longing for things to be different than they are. This is *Dukkha*.

Let me share a personal story. Several years ago, I found myself in a job that I had tirelessly pursued. I was earning a good salary, had a respected position, and was surrounded by colleagues who looked up to me. Yet, every morning, I would wake up with a heavy feeling in my heart. The work wasn't fulfilling, and I felt a constant sense of discontent. That was my first real encounter with *Dukkha*.

The Three Fires (Poisons)

Buddhism teaches us that the root cause of *Dukkha* is the Three Fires, often referred to as the Three Poisons. They are Greed, Hatred, and Delusion.

Greed (craving, desire, thirst):
Greed, in Buddhism, isn't just about wanting more money

or possessions. It's about the ceaseless craving for more - more experiences, more recognition, more happiness. It's this constant thirst that keeps us stuck in a cycle of dissatisfaction. When I was in that high-paying job, I was continually seeking the next promotion, the next big project, the next sign of success. Yet, each achievement only led to a temporary high that quickly faded, leading to more cravings.

Hatred (aversion, aggression):
Hatred, or aversion, is the other side of the coin. It's about resisting what is, pushing away what we find uncomfortable or disagreeable. It's our tendency to lash out in anger or retreat in fear when things don't go our way. I realized I was doing this when I found myself constantly complaining about my job, feeling frustrated with my colleagues, and resisting the work I had to do.

Delusion (ignorance, confusion):
The final fire is delusion, the root of the other two. Delusion is our fundamental ignorance about the way things are. It's our misguided belief that we can find lasting happiness in transient things, our confusion about what truly matters in life. In my case, I was under the delusion that success and recognition could bring me lasting happiness.

To overcome these fires, we need to cultivate their antidotes: generosity for greed, loving-kindness for hatred, and wisdom for delusion. This is the heart of the Buddhist path.

To illustrate, let's consider this section from a famous story:

"Two monks were on a pilgrimage. They came to a river where they met a beautiful young woman unable to cross. The elder monk carried her across, even though monks were forbidden to touch women. Later, the younger monk asked, 'Why did you do that?' The elder monk replied, 'I left the woman at the river. Are you still carrying her?'"

This story beautifully illustrates how our minds, clouded by delusions, often hold on to things long after their relevance has passed, causing unnecessary suffering.

Samudaya: The Truth of the Cause of Dukkha (Suffering) - Desire

"A man is but the product of his thoughts. What he thinks, he becomes." - Mahatma Gandhi. The essence of this quote is a perfect segue into the second Noble Truth of Buddhism - *Samudaya*, the origin of *Dukkha* or suffering, which is fundamentally rooted in desire.

Picture this. You're standing in front of a bakery, the aroma of freshly baked bread wafting out. Suddenly, you're overwhelmed by a strong desire for a pastry. You weren't hungry before, but now you feel a gnawing in your stomach. You buy the pastry and for a moment, you're happy. But soon after, the satisfaction wanes, and you're left wanting something else. This cycle of desire and temporary satisfaction is a core aspect of human existence.

Buddhism teaches us that the cause of our suffering is *Tanha*, often translated as 'thirst', 'desire', or 'craving'. It's the craving for sensual pleasures, for existence and non-existence, for recognition, for love, for everything that we believe will make us happy. We are driven by a constant need for more - more food, more money, more success, more validation. We get trapped in an endless cycle of desire and temporary satisfaction, followed by more desire. It's like being on a treadmill, always running but never reaching our destination because the finish line keeps moving.

But let's pause for a moment. Is desire inherently bad? After all, isn't it desire that drives us to improve, to create, to achieve? Here's where it gets interesting. Buddhism doesn't teach that desire in itself is bad. Instead, it's our attachment to these desires that cause suffering. It's when we become so entangled in our wants that we lose sight of the bigger picture and get caught up in a destructive cycle of craving and dissatisfaction.

Let's go back to the bakery example. It's not wrong to desire the pastry and enjoy it. The problem arises when we become so fixated on the pastry, so attached to the temporary pleasure it provides, that we suffer as a result. Maybe we feel guilty for indulging, or maybe we're disappointed when the pastry doesn't taste as good as we'd hoped. Our attachment to the outcome - to the idea of the pastry making us happy - is what causes suffering.

Nirodha: The Truth of the End of Dukkha (Suffering)

Mindfulness:
The cornerstone of the path. To be mindful is to be present, to observe without judgment, and to be aware of your thoughts, feelings, and the world around you. It is to live in the moment, not lost in the past or anxious about the future. A few years ago, I was caught up in a whirlwind of responsibilities. Mindfulness allowed me to step back, breathe, and appreciate the beauty of the present moment.

Discernment:
The art of understanding whether an action will be skillful or unskilful. It's about choosing the right path when confronted with crossroads. Once, I had to choose between a high-paying job that demanded long hours and a job that paid less but offered more time for personal growth and happiness. Discernment guided me to choose the latter.

Persistence:
The engine that powers your journey. It is the determination to stay on the path, despite the obstacles you might encounter. It is about never giving up. Remember Thomas Edison? He persisted through a thousand failed attempts before inventing the light bulb.

Rapture:
The joy that arises from walking the path, from seeing the fruits of your practice. It is the exhilaration of a runner nearing the finish line, the joy of an artist lost in the act of creation. Rapture is the reward for your persistence.

Serenity:
As you progress on your path, you'll find a sense of calm descending upon you. This is serenity, the peace that comes from knowing you're on the right path. It's the tranquillity of a lake at dawn, the quiet of a forest at night.

Concentration:
The ability to focus your mind, to direct your attention where you choose. Concentration is the lens that magnifies the light of mindfulness, illuminating the path ahead. It is the stillness in the eye of the storm.

Equanimity:
The final factor of awakening is equanimity. It is the ability to remain calm and balanced, regardless of the circumstances. It's the mountain that remains unmoved by the storm. Equanimity is not indifference; it's a deep understanding of the transient nature of all things.

These Seven Factors of Awakening are the keys to the end of suffering. They are not sequential but interdependent and mutually supportive. Each factor enhances and is enhanced by the others. They are like the strings of a guitar; when strummed together, they produce a harmony that leads to the symphony of enlightenment.

Magga: The Truth of the Path that Leads to the End of Dukkha (Suffering)

The Noble Eightfold Path, often referred to as the Middle Way, is the Buddhist prescription for liberating ourselves from Dukkha. It's not a strict set of rules or a rigid roadmap, but rather, it's a set of guidelines that can help us navigate life with more wisdom and compassion.

Nirvana Demystified: An Enlightened Exploration

"Enlightenment is not about becoming divine. Instead, it's about becoming more fully human..." - Lama Surya Das. With this powerful quote lighting our path, let's embark on an intellectual adventure. We're going on a journey far beyond the realm of the

mundane, where we'll unfurl the mystic concept of Nirvana.

Before we set off, let me make a confession. This confession is about Nirvana, and the fact that it had me scratching my head for years. Like a jigsaw puzzle with a thousand tiny pieces, Nirvana seemed like a concept far too grand to comprehend. Until one day, I had a revelation that allowed me to put the pieces together.

Nirvana. A word that's been thrown around, twisted, turned, and commercialized by pop culture. A term that's become as ubiquitous as a latte order at Starbucks. *"I'll have a caramel macchiato and a side of Nirvana, please!"* Funny, isn't it? Well, we're about to strip back the layers of misconception and delve into the authentic essence of Nirvana. Buckle up, because this is going to be one enlightening ride!

Nirvana, often viewed as a distant, ethereal goal, an unattainable state of pure bliss, can seem like a mountain too steep to climb. But what if I told you the mountain isn't as high as you think? What if, just what if, Nirvana was less about reaching the summit and more about appreciating the climb?

Let's challenge traditional notions of Nirvana. Let's dare to see it not as a destination but as a journey. Nirvana is not an exclusive club reserved for monks and mystics. It's a state of being that's available to you, me, and the guy who delivers the mail. It's about understanding the impermanence of life, releasing our attachments, and living fully in the present moment. Nirvana is right here, right now. You're probably thinking, *"Whoa, hold on! Are you telling me I've been holding a golden ticket all along?"* Yes, that's exactly what I'm saying!

Through the years, I've embarked on various journeys in search of Nirvana. I've sat cross-legged in meditation retreats, chanted mantras till my voice went hoarse, and even danced around a bonfire under a full moon. Some experiences were transformative, others left me with a burnt tongue from too many marshmallows. But the most profound realization was understanding that Nirvana is not an external entity, but an internal state of liberation and peace.

Now, it's your turn to explore. Here's a little exercise

Try sitting quietly for a few moments each day, letting go of your thoughts, your worries, your Instagram feed. Focus on your breath, on the present moment. Begin to notice how this simple act starts transforming your perspective.

Nirvana is not a commodity to be acquired but an experience to be lived. It's about freedom from suffering, from the endless cycle of desire and dissatisfaction. It's about embracing the now, living with purpose, and finding peace within.

Chapter Three

THE NOBLE EIGHT-FOLD PATH

"Just as the dawn is the forerunner of the arising of the sun, so true friendship is the forerunner of the arising of the noble eightfold path." - Buddha

"Peace comes from within. Do not seek it without." This beautiful aphorism from Gautama Buddha serves as a gentle reminder that the path to tranquility and enlightenment begins with our inner selves. This introspective journey is guided by the Eightfold Path, a series of principles that Buddha taught as the Middle Way to attain Nirvana.

The Eightfold Path comprises these aspects:

Right View:
Understanding the Four Noble Truths and the nature of reality.

Right Thought:
Cultivating selfless, loving, and compassionate thoughts.

Right Speech:
Speaking truthfully, kindly, and constructively.

Right Action:
Acting ethically and refraining from harmful behaviors.

Right Livelihood:
Choosing a profession that aligns with ethical principles.

Right Effort:
Consistently striving to improve oneself and cultivate positive mind-states.

Right Mindfulness:
Being fully present and aware of one's thoughts, feelings, and actions.

Right Concentration:
Developing the mental focus necessary for deep meditation.

The term 'Right' in this context, as Buddha intended, is closer to our contemporary understanding of 'appropriate' or 'wise'. These aren't dogmatic rules but guides to behavior that leads to happiness and away from suffering.

In essence, the Eightfold Path is about balance. It steers us away from the extremes of self-indulgence and self-mortification, guiding us toward a moderate, balanced path that cultivates inner peace and wisdom. This path transcends the simplistic notions of right and wrong, instead guiding us toward understanding the consequences of our actions on ourselves and others.

The Three Divisions of the Path

"*A journey of a thousand miles begins with a single step,*" said Lao Tzu, an ancient Chinese philosopher. This wisdom applies perfectly to the journey through Buddhism. In our exploration, we begin with the Three Divisions of the Path: Wisdom, Morality, and Meditation.

Wisdom, known as '*Prajna*' in Sanskrit, is the first division we encounter on this path. It's akin to the compass of our journey, directing our thoughts and actions. Right View and Right Thought, the first two elements of the Noble Eightfold Path, fall under Wisdom. Imagine yourself as the Beatles' George Harrison, who was deeply influenced by Eastern philosophy. As he sang in '*Within You Without You*', he grasped the essence of

Right View and Right Thought - seeing and understanding the interconnectedness of all things and freeing the mind of greed, hate, and delusion.

The second division, Morality or '*Sila*', is the embodiment of our wisdom in the physical world. It's the code of ethics guiding our interactions with others and the world around us. Right Speech, Right Action, and Right Livelihood constitute this division. Picture yourself as His Holiness the Dalai Lama, who personifies these principles in his daily life. He uses words to inspire, uplift, and impart wisdom (Right Speech). His actions are in the service of others and towards the preservation of peace (Right Action), and he consciously chooses a life that aligns with his spiritual beliefs (Right Livelihood).

The third division, Meditation or '*Samadhi*', is the tool that sharpens our mind and heightens our awareness. This division includes Right Effort, Right Mindfulness, and Right Concentration.

Visualize these three divisions as the spokes of a wheel - the *Dharma* Wheel. This symbolic wheel is not just any wheel. It's an emblem of Buddhist dharma, the teachings of Buddha that lead to enlightenment. Each of its eight spokes represents a step on the Noble Eightfold Path. The hub stands for moral discipline which supports the entire path, and the rim, which holds the spokes, signifies mindfulness and concentration that keep us on track.

The Dharma Wheel

The *Dharma* Wheel, also known as the *Dharmachakra*, is a symbol that represents Buddhism and Buddhist teachings. The wheel is composed of three main parts:

Hub: Represents the Three Jewels of Buddhism, which are the Buddha (the enlightened one), *Dharma* (the teachings), and *Sangha* (the community of believers).

Spokes: These represent the Eightfold Path, which are the practices that lead to enlightenment. These include Right View,

Right Intention, Right Speech, Right Action, Right Livelihood, Right Effort, Right Mindfulness, and Right Concentration.

Rim: This represents the concentration that holds everything together.

The beauty of this path lies in its balance - the Middle Way. It's neither an ascetic life of self-denial nor a hedonistic pursuit of sensory pleasures. It's a path that avoids these extremes and instead, encourages a life of moderation and mindfulness. This Middle Way leads eventually to Nirvana, the state of ultimate peace and liberation from suffering.

Following this path might feel daunting, like a journey of a thousand miles. But remember Lao Tzu's wisdom: it all begins with a single step. Your step. So, are you ready to embark on this transformative journey to Wisdom, Understanding, Loving Kindness, Compassion, Calm, and Peace.

Chapter Four

THE THREE JEWELS

"Train yourself in this way: from higher to higher, from strength to strength we will strive, and we will come to realize unsurpassed freedom." - Buddha

One of the foundational steps towards such transformation is understanding and taking refuge in the Three Jewels, namely the Buddha, *Dharma*, and *Sangha*. These are often referred to as the Three Treasures of Buddhism and serve as guiding lights on your spiritual journey. Let's delve a bit deeper into these precious treasures.

The Yellow Jewel - The Buddha

The Buddha signifies the enlightened one, the teacher who achieved ultimate wisdom and shared his knowledge with the world. It's not just the historical Buddha, Siddhartha Gautama, that we refer to here, but the Buddha nature inherent in each one of us. It's the potential for wisdom and compassion that we all possess. Taking refuge in the Buddha means recognizing and nurturing this potential.

To bring this concept to life, consider the story of American actor Keanu Reeves. Despite facing numerous personal tragedies, he found solace and strength in Buddhism. His reverence for the Buddha helped him recognize his inner potential for resilience and compassion, ultimately enabling him to lead a life of kindness and generosity. He's a living example of the Buddha nature within all of us.

The Blue Jewel - The Dharma

The *Dharma* represents the teachings of the Buddha, the truths he realized during his enlightenment. It is the path that leads to understanding and liberation from suffering. When you take refuge in the *Dharma*, you commit to following these teachings, to leading a life of mindfulness and compassion, to understanding the interconnectedness of all beings.

Think of *Dharma* as a compass guiding you through the turbulent sea of life. It's the navigation system providing you with directions to your destination - a state of peace, understanding, and liberation.

The Red Jewel - The Sangha

The *Sangha* embodies the community of fellow practitioners, those walking alongside you on the path of the *Dharma*. It is the fellowship of seekers, the support system that helps you stay the course. When you take refuge in the *Sangha*, you become part of this spiritual community, lending and receiving support, sharing experiences and learnings.

Consider the example of renowned singer Tina Turner. Despite her traumatic past, she found strength in the practice of Buddhism, particularly within her *Sangha*. Her spiritual community provided her with the necessary support and encouragement to persevere through her struggles. It's through this communal support that individuals often find the strength to continue their journey.

Taking refuge in the Three Jewels is a crucial aspect of Buddhism. It's about recognizing and nurturing your inherent potential for wisdom and compassion (Buddha), committing to a path that leads to understanding and liberation (*Dharma*), and becoming part of a supportive spiritual community (*Sangha*).

It's through this act of taking refuge that you begin your journey towards transformation, towards realizing unsurpassed freedom.

Let's review the Three Jewels once again:

1. The Buddha (Yellow Jewel): Recognizing and nurturing your inherent potential for wisdom and compassion, such as Keanu Reeves.

2. The *Dharma* (Blue Jewel): Committing to a path that leads to understanding and liberation, like a compass guiding through life.

3. The *Sangha* (Red Jewel): Becoming part of a supportive spiritual community, such as Tina Turner.

In your journey towards understanding Buddhism and integrating its principles into your life, remember these three jewels. They serve as beacons, guiding you toward a life of understanding, loving-kindness, compassion, calm, and peace.

Chapter Five

THE FIVE PRECEPTS: THE MORAL CODE

"Deeds done in harmony with one's path of life are those which bring clarity and peace and harmony to the doer."
- Buddha

"In order to carry a positive action, we must develop here a positive vision," said the Dalai Lama, an inspiring figure who has been a beacon of hope for many. This quote serves as a reminder that the foundation of our actions lies in the moral code that we follow. In Buddhism, this code is encapsulated by the Five Precepts, which form an integral part of the Noble Eightfold Path.

The Five Precepts, also known as The Five Virtues, provide a framework for ethical conduct in the world. These guiding principles are essential because they help minimize harm to yourself, the people around you, and the planet. By cultivating wisdom through the observance of these precepts, you can navigate through the chaos and uncertainty of life, finding a path to inner peace and harmony.

Let's take a closer look at the Five Precepts and explore how you can practice them in your daily life:

Abstain from Taking Life (Killing):
Practice compassion and respect for all living beings, including animals and insects. Reflect on the example of influential figures like Paul McCartney, who, inspired by his commitment to non-violence, became a staunch advocate for animal rights and vegetarianism.

Abstain from Taking What is Not Given (Stealing):
Cultivate generosity and honesty, respecting the property and belongings of others. For instance, if faced with the temptation to steal someone's idea or work, remind yourself of the importance of integrity and strive to give credit where it's due.

Abstain from Sexual Misconduct:
Honor your relationships and the relationships of others by being faithful, responsible, and respectful in all romantic and sexual encounters. Recall the story of Keanu Reeves, who has been praised for his respectful attitude towards women, both on and off the set.

Abstain from False Speech (Lying):
Practice truthfulness and sincerity, being mindful of the consequences of your words. When faced with a difficult situation, remember the wisdom of Abraham Lincoln, who once said, "No man has a good enough memory to be a successful liar."

Abstain from Intoxicants that Cloud the Mind (Drugs and Alcohol):
Foster clarity and mindfulness, avoiding substances that might impair your judgment or lead to harmful actions.

1. Abstain from Taking Life (Killing)

One of the ways in which right action is defined in Buddhism is through the Five Precepts, which serve as a moral compass guiding us in our interactions with the world. Let's delve into the first of these precepts.

The first precept, often translated as "*do not destroy life*," or "*abstain from taking life*," is about fostering a deep respect and compassion for all forms of life. In the face of this precept, we are urged to recognize the inherent value of each living being and refrain from acts that would cause harm or end a life.

This precept isn't just about avoiding physical harm; it's also about not causing emotional or psychological harm to oneself or others. It encourages us to foster an attitude of loving-kindness and compassion towards all beings, including ourselves.

Consider the example of the renowned celebrity and peace activist, Richard Gere. An ardent practitioner of Buddhism, Gere's commitment to the first precept is evident in his humanitarian work, particularly in his advocacy for human rights in Tibet and his efforts to AIDS awareness. Gere's life is an embodiment of the compassionate action urged by this precept.

Abiding by this precept can have profound implications on your mental well-being too. When you commit to not causing harm, you cultivate compassion and empathy, which can significantly reduce feelings of anger, jealousy, and resentment, contributing to your inner peace and happiness.

Here is a simple task list that can help you practice this precept in your daily life:

- Practice mindfulness to recognize and prevent harmful actions.

- Cultivate empathy by trying to understand the experiences and perspectives of others.

- Engage in acts of kindness every day.

- Reflect on your actions at the end of the day and acknowledge instances where you succeeded in upholding the precept.

2. Abstain from Taking What is Not Given (Stealing)

"In giving freedom to the slave, we assure freedom to the free - honorable alike in what we give, and what we preserve." These words by Abraham Lincoln remind us of the profound

implications of the second precept of Buddhism - do not steal.

Stealing, in its simplest form, is taking what does not belong to us. This second precept urges us to refrain from such acts, cultivating respect for the rights and possessions of others. But it's not just about the physical act of stealing. It also encompasses deceit, fraud, and any other actions that manipulate others for our benefit.

Here are some ways you can practice this precept:

- Be honest in all your dealings, ensuring you give credit where it's due.

- Respect the property of others and ask for permission before using someone else's possessions.

- Practice integrity, keeping your word, and fulfilling your promises.

Just like the first precept, the second one, too, has significant implications for your mental well-being. When you practice honesty and integrity, you nurture self-respect and peace of mind. You no longer carry the burden of guilt or fear of being found out, leading to a sense of inner freedom and tranquility.

3. Abstain from Sexual Misconduct

Sexual misconduct, in the Buddhist context, is more than just a mandate against illicit or harmful sexual behavior. It's a call for us to respect the sacredness of our bodies and the bodies of others, and to act with integrity and consideration in all matters of intimacy. By adhering to this principle, we foster trust, respect, and peace within our relationships, and we contribute to a healthier, more harmonious society.

Think about it this way - when you're mindful of your actions, you're less likely to cause harm to yourself or others. This principle holds true in various aspects of life, including your intimate relationships. Just as you exercise mindfulness in choosing your words to prevent causing emotional pain, you ought to be mindful of your actions to prevent causing harm in your romantic and sexual relationships.

In the public eye, we often see the negative impacts of sexual misconduct played out. Celebrity scandals, accusations, and the downfall of careers serve as stark reminders of the consequences of not adhering to this precept. Yet, there are also notable figures who shine a light on the path of respect and dignity.

So, how can you apply this precept in your own life?

Firstly, be clear about your intentions in any relationship. Honesty and openness pave the way for mutual understanding and respect. Secondly, always seek consent. Consent is the cornerstone of any healthy and respectful sexual relationship. And thirdly, respect the boundaries set by others. Everyone has a right to their personal space and comfort level.

4. Abstain from False Speech (Lying)

A lie, whether it takes the form of a seemingly harmless white lie or a fabricated tale meant to protect somebody, creates barriers that separate us from reality and distance us from the people in our lives. When we lie, we create a fictional world that may seem convenient in the short term but can lead to a web of complications and misunderstandings in the long run.

The precept of abstaining from lying is not just about refraining from falsehoods; it's about cultivating a love for truth, in all its forms. It's about being true to your words, true to your actions, and above all, true to yourself. It's about living authentically.

Here are some ways you can embody this precept:

- Strive for honesty in all your communications.
- Practice authenticity, being true to your feelings, thoughts, and beliefs.
- Avoid gossip and rumors, which often perpetuate untruths.

Following this precept contributes significantly to mental peace. When you speak and live your truth, you unburden yourself from the stress of maintaining untruths. You foster trust in your relationships, and most importantly, you build self-esteem, knowing that you're living authentically.

5. Do Not Become Intoxicated

"Happiness is not something ready-made. It comes from your own actions," the Dalai Lama once said. His words are a fitting segue into our exploration of the fifth precept of Buddhism: Do not become intoxicated.

Intoxication is not solely about the consumption of alcohol or drugs. It's about any substance or behavior that clouds our judgment, alters our perception of reality, or causes us to lose control over our actions. When we let ourselves become intoxicated, we distance ourselves from the clarity, mindfulness, and presence that Buddhism encourages.

Consider these practical steps to help you abide by this precept:

- Avoid excessive consumption of alcohol and refrain from using drugs.

- Monitor your consumption of media, which can also cloud judgment.

- Be mindful of behaviors that may lead to mental or emotional intoxication, such as overwork or unchecked anger.

This precept invites you to maintain clarity and control in all aspects of your life. It's not about prohibition, but about making conscious choices. It's about understanding that true happiness, contentment, and peace cannot be found in the numbness of intoxication, but in the clarity of mindfulness and presence.

Chapter Six

THE FIVE HINDRANCES

"Grasping after systems, imprisoned by dogmas for the most part is this world. But he who does not go in for system-grasping he neither doubts nor is perplexed; by not depending on others, knowledge herein comes to be his own." - Buddha

"Life is a series of natural and spontaneous changes. Don't resist them; that only creates sorrow. Let reality be reality. Let things flow naturally forward in whatever way they like," Lao Tzu. This quote perfectly encapsulates the essence of the Five Hindrances in Buddhism. These hindrances as explained below, are:

- Doubt

- Desire

- Ill Will

- Anxiousness and Worry

- Sloth and Torpor (or Laziness and Lethargy)

Doubt

The first of the Five Hindrances in Buddhism, Doubt, is a fascinating subject to delve into. It's something that all of us have experienced at some point in our lives. It's that nagging voice in your head, questioning the path you're on, the choices you've made, and even the beliefs you hold dear.

The doubt we speak of in Buddhism is not the kind that encourages critical thinking or self-reflection. It is the kind that causes us to question the teachings of the Buddha, the path to enlightenment, and our own potential to attain it. It's a crippling uncertainty that leaves us stuck, unable to move forward on our spiritual journey.

You see, doubt has this uncanny ability to creep into our minds, often unnoticed. It's like a fog that rolls in, obscuring our vision and causing us to lose sight of our destination. It's a hindrance that can easily derail our spiritual progress if left unchecked.

Take, for example, the story of Thomas Edison. Edison was a prolific inventor, holding 1,093 patents for his inventions. Yet, his journey was not without challenges. His most notable invention, the electric light bulb, took him 1,000 attempts before he finally succeeded. Now, imagine if Edison had succumbed to doubt on his 999th attempt. We might still be living in a world lit by candlelight!

In Buddhism, overcoming doubt doesn't mean blind faith. It means developing a deep understanding of the teachings and seeing their truth through your own experience. It's about finding your own proof of the path's efficacy.

Desire

Desire, in its purest form, is a powerful motivator. It's the driving force that propels us to chase our dreams, strive for success, and seek fulfillment in our lives. However, when desire becomes unbalanced or misdirected, it can transform into a hindrance, a stumbling block on our path to spiritual growth and enlightenment. This is especially true in the context of Buddhism, where desire is considered one of the Five Hindrances to spiritual development.

It's a thirst for something that is not present, a longing for something more. This craving can manifest in many forms, from material possessions to relationships, status, or experiences. When we're caught in the grip of *tanha*, we're constantly seeking fulfillment outside of ourselves, believing that the next promotion, the next purchase, or the next relationship will finally bring us the happiness we seek.

However, the truth is that this type of desire only leads to suffering. It's like a mirage in the desert, always appearing just out of reach, no matter how far we travel. The more we chase after it, the more it eludes us. This is the first hindrance on the path to enlightenment in Buddhism.

So, how do we overcome this hindrance? The answer lies in understanding the nature of desire and learning to navigate it with wisdom and mindfulness.

First, it's important to recognize that desire, in and of itself, is not inherently bad. It's a natural part of the human experience. The problem arises when our desires become attachments, leading us to perceive our happiness as contingent on external possessions or circumstances.

To overcome this, we must learn to cultivate non-attachment. This doesn't mean that we should abandon all our desires and live a life devoid of ambition or enjoyment. Rather, it means learning to hold our desires lightly, understanding that they are not the source of our happiness.

Practicing mindfulness can be a powerful tool in this process. When we're mindful, we're fully present in the moment, not lost in thoughts about the past or the future. This allows us to see our desires for what they truly are: transient thoughts and feelings that come and go. We can observe them without getting caught up in them, without allowing them to dictate our actions or our sense of self-worth.

Let's take a moment to reflect on this with a simple mindfulness exercise:

- Take a few deep breaths, bringing your attention to the present moment.

- Bring to mind a desire that you've been struggling with recently.

- Observe this desire without judgment. Notice how it feels in your body. What thoughts or emotions does it bring up?

- Remind yourself that this desire is not you. It's just a thought, a feeling. It doesn't define or control you.

- Let go of the desire, allowing it to pass like a cloud in the sky.

Ill Will

Ill will, the next of the Five Hindrances in Buddhism, is another obstacle that we must learn to overcome on our journey toward enlightenment. This emotion, which can manifest as anger, resentment, or hostility, acts as a powerful roadblock, preventing us from experiencing the peace and tranquility that come with mindfulness and meditation.

Let's consider a real-world example. Remember the famous feud between Steve Jobs and Bill Gates? These titans of technology, both geniuses in their own right, allowed their rivalry to escalate into personal animosity. This ill will not only caused them personal distress but also led to missed opportunities for collaboration that could have further revolutionized the tech world.

Such is the power of ill will. It blinds us to opportunities, isolates us from others, and keeps us stuck in a cycle of negativity.

But the good news is, we can overcome it. Here's how:

- **Practice mindfulness:** By becoming more aware of your thoughts and feelings, you can identify ill will as it arises and choose not to engage with it.

- **Develop compassion:** Instead of responding to others with anger or hostility, try to understand their perspective and respond with kindness.

- **Forgive:** Holding onto grudges only fuels ill will. By forgiving others—and yourself—you can let go of negative feelings and move forward.

- **Cultivate positivity:** Make a conscious effort to focus on the good in others and in yourself. This can help counteract the negativity that comes with ill will.

- **Meditate:** Regular meditation can help you manage negative emotions and cultivate a sense of inner peace.

"Holding on to anger is like grasping a hot coal with the intent of throwing it at someone else; you are the one who gets burned."
— Buddha

Anxiousness and Worry

Anxiety and worry, the penultimate of the Five Hindrances, often stir up a storm in our minds and can be especially challenging to overcome. I'd like to share a personal story that might resonate with you. There was a period in my life when the future was uncertain, and my mind was filled with a whirlwind of "what ifs" and worst-case scenarios. I worried incessantly, losing precious sleep and peace of mind. It was during this time that I recognized the profound hold anxiety and worry had over me.

You may have experienced this too. Perhaps you've found yourself lying awake at night, fretting over an upcoming event or an unresolved issue. Or perhaps your mind often races with worries about the future, to the extent that you struggle to be present in the moment.

Anxiousness and worry can form a formidable barrier to our spiritual progress. They disturb our peace of mind, create unnecessary stress, and prevent us from fully engaging with our meditation practice. However, like the other Hindrances, they are not insurmountable obstacles but challenges to be understood and overcome.

Here's a list summarizing a few strategies to help manage anxiousness and worry:

- Observing our thoughts and feelings without judgment through mindfulness can help us avoid engaging with worry.

- Intentionally focusing on positive thoughts and emotions can counterbalance negativity brought about by worry.

- Exercise can reduce anxiety and promote well-being.

- Seeking support from trusted individuals or mental health professionals can provide helpful coping strategies and perspective.

- Regular meditation can improve our ability to remain present and avoid getting carried away by anxious thoughts.

Let's remember the Buddha's words: *"There is no path to happiness: happiness is the path."* Anxiousness and worry can be seen as teachers rather than enemies, helping us recognize the areas in our lives that need attention or change. They provide us with the opportunity to cultivate patience, resilience, and compassion toward ourselves.

Sloth and Torpor (Laziness and Lethargy)

These roadblocks can be particularly insidious as they subtly sap our energy and motivation, preventing us from fully engaging with our meditation practice and life itself.

Remember the story of the tortoise and the hare? The hare, despite being the faster and more capable animal, loses the race because he chooses to rest and procrastinate, while the tortoise, though slower, wins because of his consistent effort and refusal to succumb to laziness. In the same way, we often have all the skills and capabilities we need to achieve our spiritual goals, but we are held back by our own inertia.

Sloth and torpor can manifest in various ways. We might find ourselves feeling physically sluggish, mentally foggy, or emotionally drained. We may start avoiding our meditation practice or find our minds wandering aimlessly when we do try to meditate. These are all signs that sloth and torpor have crept in.

The good news is, we are not powerless against these hindrances.

Here's how you can tackle them:

- **Set clear goals:** Having a clear vision of what we want to achieve can help us stay motivated and focused.

- **Establish a routine:** Regular practice can help us build momentum and make it easier to stick with our meditation.

- **Take care of our physical health:** Regular exercise, a healthy diet, and enough sleep can help keep our energy levels high.

- **Seek support:** Joining a meditation group or finding a mentor can provide us with the encouragement and accountability we need.

- **Practice mindfulness:** By being aware of our thoughts and feelings, we can notice when sloth and torpor start to creep in and take steps to counteract them.

Chapter Seven

THE FOUR IMMEASURABLES

"There are four bases of sympathy: charity, kind speech, doing a good turn and treating all alike." - Buddha

The Four Immeasurables:

- Loving-Kindness
- Compassion
- Sympathetic Joy
- Equanimity

"Thousands of candles can be lighted from a single candle, and the life of the candle will not be shortened. Happiness never decreases by being shared." — Buddha

Loving-Kindness (Metta)

It was on a cold winter's day while I was huddled in the warmth of my study that I received an email. It was from a complete stranger living halfway across the globe. The message was simple, *"I hope this email finds you well. I just wanted to say*

I appreciate your work and I hope you have a lovely day." This small act of kindness is a beautiful illustration of the Buddhist concept of *Metta*, also known as loving-kindness.

Metta is a Pali term that doesn't have an exact English equivalent, but it can be described as benevolent kindness towards all beings without exception. It's not selective; it doesn't differentiate between a friend, an enemy, or a stranger. *Metta* is a boundless, universal love — an aspiration, a potency of the heart.

When we cultivate *Metta* within ourselves, we begin to dissolve the barriers that we've erected due to fear, jealousy, or hatred. We start to see beyond the labels of 'friend', 'enemy', or 'stranger'. We begin to wish for the well-being of all life forms, irrespective of who they are, where they come from, or what they've done. This may sound like a Herculean task, but it's surprisingly natural once we start practicing it.

Here's a simple *Metta* meditation exercise you can start with:

- Find a quiet place and sit comfortably.

- Close your eyes and take a few deep breaths to center yourself.

- Begin by directing *Metta* towards yourself. Silently repeat, *"May I be happy. May I be healthy. May I be safe. May I live with ease."*

- Next, think of a person you love. Direct the same wishes towards them.

- Think of a neutral person, someone you neither like nor dislike. Extend the same wishes to them.

- Now, think of someone with whom you have a difficult relationship. If you're ready, try extending *Metta* to them as well.

- Finally, expand this wish to all beings everywhere, *"May all beings be happy. May all beings be healthy. May all beings be safe. May all beings live with ease."*

This practice may not be easy at first, especially when directing *Metta* towards people we have difficulties with. But remember, *Metta* is a practice. It's like exercising a muscle. The more we do it, the stronger it becomes.

Cultivating *Metta* is a powerful way to transform our hearts and minds. It allows us to move from a space of separateness and fear to a space of connectedness and love. It's the first step towards embracing the four immeasurable qualities that are the foundation of a truly enriched life.

Compassion (Karuna)

"Compassion is not a gesture of the weak, but the fortitude of the strong." This quote from the renowned Buddhist monk, Matthieu Ricard, perfectly encapsulates the essence of compassion, or *Karuna*, in Buddhism. It's a cornerstone of our practice, and it is not simply about feeling sorry for others; it's about the profound desire to alleviate suffering wherever it exists. Let's delve into this immeasurable aspect and understand how it can transform your life and mental well-being.

Compassion (*Karuna*), in its simplest terms, is the heart's response to suffering. It's the empathetic understanding that perceives the struggle of others and wishes to alleviate it. But compassion isn't just about acknowledging pain and suffering. It also involves a commitment to taking action to relieve it. When we cultivate compassion, we're not only acknowledging the universal truth of suffering but also committing ourselves to alleviate it.

In my personal journey with Buddhism, I've found that cultivating compassion isn't always easy, particularly when we encounter people or situations that challenge our patience and understanding. Yet, it's in these moments that compassion becomes an invaluable tool for personal transformation and peace.

This is the transformative power of compassion. It not only changes our perspective but also alters our reactions, leading to greater peace and equanimity in our lives.

But how can you cultivate such compassion? Here's a practical guide to help you:

- **Mindfulness:** Start by practicing mindfulness. Be fully present in each moment and allow yourself to fully perceive the experiences and emotions of others.

- **Empathy:** Try to understand the feelings and perspectives of others. Put yourself in their shoes and try to feel what they are feeling. This understanding is the first step toward developing compassion.

- **Action:** Compassion involves more than just understanding; it also requires action. Look for ways to alleviate the suffering of others, whether it's lending a listening ear, offering help, or simply being there for them.

- **Meditation:** Compassion meditation, also known as Metta or Loving-Kindness Meditation, is a powerful tool for cultivating compassion. It involves consciously sending wishes of well-being, happiness, and peace to all beings.

"When you begin to touch your heart or let your heart be touched, you begin to discover that it's bottomless, that it doesn't have any resolution, that this heart is huge, vast, and limitless. You begin to discover how much warmth and gentleness is there, as well as how much space." - Pema Chödrön.

Compassion, in essence, is about opening our hearts to the suffering of others and ourselves. It's about acknowledging this suffering and taking steps to alleviate it. As you walk this path of compassion, you'll find a profound sense of peace and fulfillment pervading your life, transforming your experiences and interactions in remarkable ways. Remember, compassion isn't just for the benefit of others; it's equally for our own mental and emotional well-being. Embrace *Karuna* and let its transformative power guide you on your path to enlightenment.

Sympathetic Joy (Mudita)

The Dalai Lama once said, "If you want others to be happy, practice compassion. If you want to be happy, practice compassion." But there's another aspect of Buddhist philosophy that contributes to happiness, both ours and that of others, and that's sympathetic joy, or *Mudita*.

Sympathetic joy is the genuine joy we feel at the happiness and success of others. It's the ability to take sincere delight in the achievements, well-being, and joy of others, without a hint of jealousy or resentment. It's about celebrating others as we would celebrate our own success.

But why is *Mudita* so important? Well, it's because it helps us escape the trap of jealousy and resentment. These negative emotions not only cloud our minds but also lead to a significant amount of suffering. By cultivating *Mudita*, we can let go of these destructive emotions and replace them with happiness and contentment.

Now, you might be thinking, "That sounds great, but how do I actually practice Mudita?" The answer lies in mindfulness, empathy, and conscious effort.

Here's a simple guide to help you get started:

- **Mindfulness:** Be present in each moment and notice the joy and success of others. Pay attention to their happiness and allow yourself to feel joy for them.

- **Empathy:** Put yourself in their shoes. Understand what their success or happiness means to them and share in their joy.

- **Conscious Effort:** *Mudita* doesn't always come naturally, especially if we're used to feelings of jealousy or resentment. Make a conscious effort to celebrate the joy of others, even if it feels difficult at first.

- **Meditation:** Practice *Mudita* meditation. This involves consciously generating feelings of joy for the happiness of others.

Let me share a personal anecdote to illustrate the transformative power of *Mudita*. A few years ago, a friend of mine achieved significant success in her career, a field similar to mine. Initially, I felt a pang of jealousy. I felt as if her success somehow diminished my own achievements. But then, I remembered the teachings of Buddhism, and I decided to cultivate *Mudita* instead. I took a moment to genuinely appreciate her hard work and dedication, and I felt a profound sense of joy at her success. Not only did this shift in perspective free me from negative emotions, but it also deepened my friendship with her.

"A moment of self-compassion can change your entire day. A string of such moments can change the course of your life." - Christopher Germer

Equanimity (Uppekha)

"Equanimity is the hallmark of spirituality. It is neither chasing nor avoiding but just being in the middle." - Amit Ray

Uppekha, the last of the four Immeasurables, is often misunderstood as indifference or disinterest. But that couldn't be further from the truth. Equanimity isn't about not caring; it's about inner balance. It's about being able to navigate life's ups and downs with a steady heart and a calm mind.

Imagine you're a sailor out on the vast ocean. Sometimes the sea is calm and other times it's stormy. If you panic every time a storm hits or get too attached to the calm periods, you'll likely have a difficult journey. But if you maintain your composure, if you're able to sail through both the calm and the storm with the same steadiness, you're practicing *Uppekha*.

Practicing equanimity doesn't mean you won't experience joy, sadness, pleasure, or pain. These are natural responses to the world around us. What it does mean is that you won't be swayed by these experiences. You'll feel them, acknowledge them, but they won't throw you off balance.

Here's a simple practice to cultivate equanimity:

- Sit quietly and take a few deep breaths.

- Bring to mind a situation that you're currently struggling with.

- Acknowledge any emotions that arise. Don't judge them or push them away. Simply notice them.

- Now, silently repeat to yourself, "Things are as they are. This is what's happening right now. It's okay to feel this way."

- Let go of any desire to change or control the situation. Simply allow it to be as it is.

- Notice any shifts in your emotions or thoughts. Remember, the goal isn't to eliminate the discomfort but to find steadiness amidst it.

Chapter Eight

MEDITATION AND MINDFULNESS

"All experience is preceded by mind, led by mind, made by mind." - *Buddha*

Meditation

"Life is a dance. Mindfulness is witnessing that dance." - Amit Ray. Let's take a moment to reflect on this quote. It's a simple yet profound statement that captures the essence of meditation. Now, let's explore the transformative power of meditation in the context of Buddhism.

Meditation is not just a practice; it's a journey, a path to self-discovery. It's like a mirror that reflects our inner selves, helping us understand who we truly are. It's a tool that helps us navigate the tumultuous seas of life with grace and equanimity.

Shinzen Young, a renowned meditation teacher, beautifully encapsulates the benefits of mindful meditation into three core elements: sensory clarity, concentration, and equanimity. Let's delve a little deeper into each of these.

Sensory clarity is about being fully aware of what we're experiencing in the present moment. It's about tuning into our senses and observing our thoughts, emotions, and physical sensations without judgment. It's like turning up the volume on life, experiencing it in high-definition.

Concentration, on the other hand, is about focus. It's about training our minds to stay in the present moment, not getting lost in the past or the future. It's about cultivating a sense of stillness amidst the chaos of life.

Equanimity is perhaps the most profound of the three. It's about developing a balanced mind, a mind that remains undisturbed in the face of life's ups and downs. It's about learning to ride the waves of life with grace and poise.

Now, let's take a step back and look at the bigger picture. In the grand tapestry of Buddhism, meditation is a vibrant thread that weaves through its philosophical system. It's an antidote to the nagging difficulties of ego, a pathway to transformation. It's a beacon of light for those seeking to live a life free of greed, hate, and illusion.

In the Pali canon, the Buddha outlines two meditative qualities that are mutually supportive: *samatha*, or "calm," and *vipassanā*, or "insight." Picture these qualities as a pair of swift messengers, working in harmony to deliver the profound message of Nirvana.

Samatha, the first messenger, brings calm. It's like a soothing balm for our restless minds, helping us cultivate a sense of peace and tranquility. *Vipassanā*, the second messenger, brings insight. It's like a sharp sword that cuts through the veil of ignorance, helping us see reality as it truly is.

Together, these two messengers deliver the profound message of nirvana, the ultimate goal of Buddhism. Nirvana is not a place but a state of mind. It's a state of profound peace and happiness, free from the shackles of greed, hate, and delusion.

Now, let's take this knowledge and put it into practice.

Here's a simple mindfulness exercise to get you started:

- Find a quiet place where you won't be disturbed.
- Sit comfortably, with your back straight but not stiff.
- Close your eyes and take a few deep breaths.
- Bring your attention to your breath. Notice the sensation of the breath coming in and going out.
- If your mind wanders, gently bring it back to the breath.
- Continue this practice for a few minutes each day.

Remember, meditation is not about achieving a certain state or having a particular experience. It's about being present, being fully engaged with whatever is happening right now. It's about cultivating a sense of curiosity and openness toward our own experience.

Some Forms of Meditation

Here's the thing: meditation is not just about sitting cross-legged on a mat, murmuring '*Om*' in a low voice until your throat dries up. No, meditation is a lot more varied and exciting than you might think. And I'm going to walk you through a few forms of meditation that are as soothing as a warm cup of chamomile tea on a frosty winter evening.

First on the list is *Vipassanā*. Originating from the land of the Buddha, *Vipassanā* is one of the most ancient forms of meditation. It focuses on seeing things as they truly are. It's all about observing the reality within yourself, and let me tell you, once you start peeling back those layers, it's like finding a never-ending Russian nesting doll!

Next, we have *Samatha*. If you think this sounds like a soft, soothing lullaby, you're not far off. This form of meditation involves calming the mind and its 'formations.' It's like giving your thoughts a tranquilizer so that you can experience peace. It might seem a bit challenging at first, but once you get the hang of it, it's smoother than a hot knife through butter.

51

Following *Samatha*, we have Mantra Meditation. This form of meditation uses a repeated sound, phrase, or word to clear the mind. Imagine you're in the serene valleys of Tibet, surrounded by lush greenery, and you're chanting *"Om mani padme hum,"* which loosely translates to *"Hail to the jewel in the lotus."* Believe me, it's a cathartic experience that just melts away your stress.

Next, we have *Metta* Meditation, also known as Loving-Kindness Meditation. This form of meditation is all about directing good vibes toward yourself and others. It's like sending out a boomerang of love and positive energy and watching it circle back to you.

Lastly, there is Chanting, Visualization, and Walking Meditations. Each offers a distinct flavor, akin to a variety of chocolates in a box. Chanting is all about using rhythmic spoken or sung words to get into a meditative state. Visualization is like going on a mental vacation, creating serene images in your mind, and walking meditation is about being mindful of every step and every breath while taking a peaceful stroll.

Here's a little exercise for you. I want you to pick one form of meditation from the list above that resonates with you the most. Try practicing it for five minutes each day for the next week. Write down any changes or feelings you notice in your thoughts, behavior, or emotions in a journal. This exercise will not only give you a hands-on experience with meditation but also give you insight into how it affects you.

I can tell you from personal experience that the impact of meditation is like adding a splash of vibrant color to a black and white painting. It's the extra seasoning in the soup of life that enhances its flavor and makes it worth savoring. And the beauty of it all? Anyone can learn to meditate - it's as universal as the air we breathe, the water we drink, and the love we share.

Meditation Equipment

"Tools make the man," so goes a modern adaptation of a proverb. But when it comes to meditation, I am inclined to make a slight amendment: *"The lack of tools can make the man, but having*

them doesn't hurt." Let me explain.

As we embark on the journey into the serene world of Buddhism, it is essential to remember that meditation is a sojourn of the mind. It does not necessarily require physical apparatus. But just as a wanderer appreciates a map or a compass, there are certain tools, traditionally used by many practicing Buddhists, that could enhance your meditation experience. However, these differ among the various schools of Buddhism and are not prerequisites. You see, meditation is a no-frills affair; it's like showing up to a potluck with just your appetite!

Now, for those of you who like a little extra, let's dive into this fascinating array of meditation equipment.

1. A Meditation Cushion (Zafu)

Imagine being in the middle of a deeply profound meditation session, but all you can focus on is your sore bottom. That's where the Zafu comes in! This meditation cushion, often filled with kapok or buckwheat, provides a soft and stable platform for you to perch upon. It's like sitting on a cloud, without the fear of falling through!

2. Incense

Incense sticks have a rather quaint and practical use in meditation - they serve as timers. In the old days, meditators would start their session when the incense was lit and would know it was time to wrap up when the sweet-smelling smoke stopped wafting through the air. It's like a gentle, olfactory tap on the shoulder, reminding you of the world outside your mind. Plus, the aroma can help create a calming environment.

3. Timer, Bell, or Tibetan Singing Bowl

Timers, bells, and Tibetan singing bowls create an auditory backdrop for meditation. Like a gentle ripple breaking the surface of a calm lake, the resonating sound of these instruments serves as a sonic marker for the start and end of your meditation session.

4. Altar and Altar Cloth

An altar adorned with a special cloth can serve as a visual reminder of your commitment to practice. It is a little corner in your home dedicated to your spiritual journey, a constant reminder of the tranquil path you have chosen.

5. Candles and Flowers

In the dance of shadows cast by a flickering candle, we see the symbol of the light of truth, guiding us through obscurity. Similarly, flowers, in their ephemeral beauty, remind us of the impermanence of nature. Together, they form a compelling, tactile metaphor for some of the fundamental teachings of Buddhism.

6. Devotional Objects

Statues of Buddha or other devotional objects on your altar can serve as focal points during meditation. They represent the enlightened state you aspire to attain. It's like having a snapshot of your destination, a gentle nudge reminding you of your journey's goal.

7. Prayer Beads

Finally, prayer beads, often carved from the wood of the Bodhi tree. A strand typically contains 108 beads and is used in the practice of Japa, where you repeat a mantra, like "*Om mani padme hum.*" The beads help you keep track of the number of repetitions, like a spiritual abacus.

Now, here's a little exercise for you:

Create a space for meditation in your home, using any of the items mentioned above that resonate with you. Don't fret if you can't get all of them - remember, the most crucial tool for meditation is your mind. This setup is simply a way to enhance your experience.

Posture

Ah, posture! It's a deceptively simple concept, isn't it? We've all been admonished as kids to *"Sit up straight!"* But who knew that this seemingly mundane directive could evolve into an intricate dance with profound implications for the mind, body, and spirit?

As we delve into meditation, it's essential to know that posture isn't about rigid adherence to an esoteric protocol, but rather an understanding of our bodies and the interconnectedness of our physical and mental well-being. In the realm of meditation, the body is not merely a vehicle, but an active participant in the journey to inner peace.

Let's start with a story. Once upon a time, in my early days of learning about Buddhism and meditation, I was convinced that I had to master the full lotus posture. You know the one - with both feet resting on the opposite thigh, like a pretzel. The only problem was that my body, being more accustomed to ergonomic office chairs and plush sofas, did not quite agree. The harder I tried, the more my knees screamed for mercy. It was quite the standoff, my stubbornness against my body's unwillingness to bend to my will. I learned a crucial lesson from this experience: the journey toward mindfulness begins with listening to our bodies, respecting their boundaries, and meeting them where they are.

So, let's explore some postures that may be more agreeable to your knees, shall we?

The full lotus: It's the quintessential meditation pose, with each foot resting on the opposite thigh. It's excellent for stability and alignment, but be warned, it's not for everyone, and that's okay!

The half-lotus: This one is a bit less pretzel-like. One foot rests on the opposite thigh, and the other rests below the thigh. It's a bit easier but still offers good stability.

The Burmese style: This is the grounded version of the lotus. Both feet rest on the ground in front of you, with one leg in front of the other. It's comfortable and very accommodating for those who, like me, have bodies that draw the line at pretzel impersonations.

Seated on a straight-backed chair: This one is for the rebels who refuse to sit on the floor. Make sure your feet touch the ground, your back is straight but not rigid, and your hands resting on your knees or lap.

Remember that the perfect posture is the one where you can maintain a straight but relaxed back, and your body isn't distracting you with complaints of discomfort. It should enable you, not hinder you.

Now, here's a helpful tip. Doing some light stretching before settling into your posture can make a world of difference. It's like giving your body a heads-up, *"Hey, we're about to do this mindfulness thing."* This not only helps to prevent discomfort but also serves as a transition ritual, a bridge from the hustle and bustle of daily life to the calm space of meditation.

Lastly, remember to respect your body and its limits. Just as there is no one 'right' way to seek inner peace, there is no one 'right' posture. It's a personal journey, and the ideal posture is the one that allows you to travel the path of mindfulness with comfort and dignity. Your body is your partner in this journey, and like all good partners, it deserves to be heard and respected.

Alright, now that you've had this crash course in meditation posture, I hope you feel prepared to sit (literally) with your practice. Remember, the only 'bad' meditation posture is the one that causes you discomfort or harm. Your body is wise. Listen to it, and it will guide you well.

Environment

Ah, there's no place like home. Or is there? Home, office, outdoors - wherever you are, a tranquil environment can make all the difference to your day. Especially when you're trying to meditate. In fact, it's extremely essential. Let me explain. Picture this: you're meditating, zenning out, when suddenly, a loud car honks outside your window. Or worse, your phone buzzes with another notification. It's like someone splashing cold water on your face while you're in a warm, soothing bath.

So, let's make your environment meditation-friendly. First things first, find a quiet spot where the chaos of the world can't intrude. This could be a nook in your home, a cozy corner in your office, or even a park bench. It's not so much about where you are, as it is about the peace the place can provide.

But even in the quietest corners, time has a sneaky way of slipping away from us, doesn't it? One minute, you're taking deep, calming breaths, and the next, you're wondering if you've been sitting there for an eternity. So, here's a handy tip - set a time limit. Maybe you start with ten minutes, like dipping your toes into a pool to test the waters. Then, as you grow more comfortable and your focus improves, you can gradually increase this limit.

Now, when it comes to timers, I want you to imagine the most abrupt, jarring alarm you've ever heard. Got it? Great. Now forget it. You're not using that for your meditation. Instead, find a sound that is as gentle and soothing as a lullaby. Trust me, you don't want to be jolted out of your serene state.

One last thing - when your timer does eventually sing its soft melody, don't just leap up. Remember, you've been sitting for a while. Your legs might be a bit stiff or even asleep. So, take your time. Stand up slowly, and shake out your legs. There's no rush. You're in the zen zone now, remember?

Here's a little extra something you can do. Just as you're about to end your meditation session, you could perform a simple act of honor - a bow. It could be a physical one, or just in your heart. It's a moment of reverence for the practice you've just completed.

Your meditation environment is just like your mind - it should be peaceful, devoid of distractions, and conducive to mindfulness. Now go on, make that perfect space for yourself. Your future zen-self will thank you.

The Breath

Can I share a little secret with you? It's something we all share, something that's right under our noses (literally!) - yet, we often overlook it.

Yes, it's your breath.

Your breath is one of the most reliable allies you can have in your journey of life. Always there, faithfully following your rhythm, in sorrow and joy, in haste and rest. It's the most loyal companion you could ever wish for. Yet, we barely pay attention to it. In our fast-paced lives, where we constantly juggle work, family, and that seemingly never-ending to-do list, it's easy to forget about this ever-present partner.

Consider this scenario: You're frantically racing through your day, and suddenly you feel the world spinning around you. Your heart's pounding, you're gasping for breath, panic creeping in. In those moments, you realize the power of your breath, and you gasp, trying to draw in more air. That's when your breath says, *"Hey there, I've been here all along, just breathe!"*

Just like a trusty friend who pulls you aside and says, *"Take a moment, breathe, everything's going to be okay,"* your breath is always there for you. You need only turn your awareness to it.

In the teachings of Buddhism, the awareness of breath plays a crucial role. It forms the foundation of Buddhist-style meditation, allowing you to anchor your consciousness and find a steady space amidst the storm of thoughts and emotions. Breath, in Buddhism, is more than a physical process; it's a metaphorical bridge connecting your body and mind.

Now, there are as many ways to focus on the breath as there are to cook an egg (and trust me, that's quite a few). From *pranayama*, which is part of the yogic tradition, to *Zazen*, the Zen meditation style, to *Anapanasati*, which means mindfulness of breathing in Pali - the ancient language of early Buddhist scriptures.

Pranayama is a Sanskrit word that translates to "life-force control." It consists of various techniques that influence the flow of energy in your body by controlling your breath. In contrast, *Zazen*, which means "seated meditation" in Japanese, is the practice of seeking the "just sitting" state, where your breath becomes your focal point of awareness. Then there's *Anapanasati*, a practice that Buddha himself is said to have taught. In this method, your focus is on the sensations of breathing, observing it without trying to control it.

Regardless of the method you choose, these techniques share a common goal - enhancing your awareness and understanding of your breath. By harnessing the power of your breath, you can tap into the tranquility it offers, thereby bringing peace and calmness to your chaotic life.

For starters, let's take a simple exercise. Wherever you are, whatever you're doing, pause for a moment. Now, close your eyes, take a slow, deep breath in, hold it for a second, and then exhale slowly. Repeat this for a few more breaths. As you do so, observe your breath - feel the cool air entering your nostrils, your chest expanding, and then the warm air leaving your body.

How did that feel? Simple, wasn't it? That's the power of breath awareness. It doesn't need any fancy props or dedicated time. You can do it right here, right now.

Mindfulness

Mindfulness. What a treasure trove it holds within! You've heard the term thrown around before, haven't you? Perhaps, in the midst of your frenetic everyday rush, it came to you as a distant echo, a whisper of a better way. Or maybe you heard it during your brief ventures into the realm of self-improvement, nestled snugly between promises of tranquility, stress relief, and that elusive unicorn – happiness. But what is mindfulness really? And what does it have to do with emotional intelligence and the principles of Buddhism? Well, we're about to embark on a journey of discovery together to find out.

Imagine you're on a wild river ride. The water is churning, swirling, and you're in a small boat, holding on for dear life. The river is your life, the whirlpools and currents are your emotions, and the boat... well, the boat is you. In this chaotic scenario, mindfulness is the sturdy oar you wield. It helps you navigate, dodge the whirlpools, and avoid capsizing. Mindfulness is being present in the here and now, acknowledging the water's fury but not allowing it to dictate your direction.

John D Mayer, Peter Salovey, and David R Caruso, the dynamic trio who brought emotional intelligence (EI) into the limelight, divided EI into four integral components. These are: accurately detecting emotions in oneself and others, using emotions to facilitate thinking, understanding emotions and their language, and finally, managing emotions to fulfill certain aims. It sounds like quite a handful, doesn't it? But hold on, don't let it overwhelm you. That's where mindfulness and meditation step in.

The practice of mindfulness and meditation is an invaluable tool in your emotional toolkit. It aids in the development of empathy and emotional control, two key components of emotional intelligence. With mindfulness, you learn to recognize your emotions, understand them, and not be swayed by their tempest. Think about it – it's like having your own internal weather report!

Now, let's take a detour and visit the cradle of mindfulness – Buddhism. The concept of 'mindfulness' in Buddhism is akin to 'recollection' or 'remembering.' An interesting take, isn't it? But don't mistake it for a trip down memory lane. It's not about dwelling on past events, but rather remembering to stay rooted in the present moment. As Dr Bhikkhu Analayo says, it's *"complete awareness of the current moment"* that enhances and develops memory.

Indian Buddhist scholar Asanga described mindfulness as the mind's ability to not forget the object experienced. The aim? To prevent distraction. Imagine your mind as a focused lens, clear and unclouded by stray thoughts or emotions. Sounds like quite the superpower, doesn't it?

Let's dive a little deeper into the practices of mindfulness within Buddhism. There are several exercises, like the four *Satipaṭṭhānas,* or 'establishments of mindfulness', and *Ānāpānasati,* the 'mindfulness of breathing'. *Sampajañña,* or 'clear comprehension', is another skill frequently associated with mindfulness. It's the ability to understand what one is doing, what's happening in the mind, and whether it's being influenced by unwholesome factors.

I invite you to take a moment to pause. Close your eyes and focus on your breath, the in and out, the rise and fall of your chest. That's it! You're already practicing mindfulness, taking the first step on this incredible journey. This is the essence of mindfulness – a simple, yet profoundly transformative act.

Chapter Nine

KARMA AND REBIRTH

"Better than a hundred years lived in ignorance, without contemplation, is one single day of life lived in wisdom and deep contemplation." - Buddha

Karma is not a difficult idea

Now, let's dive into one of the most misunderstood concepts in Buddhism: Karma.

You know, I often smile when I hear people use the term "karma" in everyday conversation. It's usually something along the lines of, *"Oh, that's karma for you!"* when someone gets their just desserts. But karma is so much more than cosmic payback.

In its simplest form, karma is the law of cause and effect. It's the idea that every action has a consequence, and these consequences shape our lives. It's like throwing a pebble into a pond. The pebble is your action, and the ripples it creates are the effects of that action.

Understanding and applying the concept of karma is not as difficult as it seems. It's about being mindful of our actions and their effects on ourselves and others. It's about making conscious choices that lead to positive outcomes.

Now, here's a little exercise for you:

Over the next week, I want you to pay close attention to your actions and their consequences. Write them down in a journal. At the end of the week, review your entries. You might be surprised at what you find.

Remember, karma is not a punishment or reward. It's a tool for understanding the interconnectedness of our actions and their effects. It's a path to a more mindful and compassionate life. And it's a path that's open to everyone.

Common Misunderstandings About Karma

First off, let's clear up a common misconception. Karma is not some cosmic scorekeeper, tallying up your good and bad deeds, ready to reward or punish you accordingly. If you're imagining a celestial accountant with a giant ledger, erase that image from your mind. Karma doesn't work that way.

Think of Karma as more like a seed. Every action you take is a seed you plant. Some seeds grow into beautiful flowers, others into thorny bushes. The kind of seed you plant, through your actions, will determine what grows in your life.

Now, I know what you're thinking, *"are you saying if I do good things, only good things will happen to me?"* Well, not exactly. Life is complex, and so is Karma. It's not a one-to-one transaction. But generally, positive actions create conditions for positive outcomes, and negative actions create conditions for negative outcomes.

But here's the beautiful thing about Karma. You can change the seeds you're planting. When I started taking care of my health, meditating, and practicing mindfulness, I began planting seeds of self-care. And guess what? Those seeds grew into a garden of well-being.

So, let's try a little exercise:

- Think about the seeds you're planting in your life right now.

- Are they seeds of kindness, compassion, and understanding?

- Or are they seeds of anger, resentment, and neglect?

- Remember, you have the power to choose what seeds you plant.

- Here's a task list to help you along the way:

- Identify the seeds: What actions are you taking in your life right now? Are they positive or negative?

- Choose your seeds: Decide what kind of actions you want to take. What kind of seeds do you want to plant?

- Plant your seeds: Start taking those actions. Plant those seeds.

- Nurture your seeds: Keep taking positive actions. Nurture those seeds with mindfulness and compassion.

Remember, Karma is not about punishment or reward. It's about understanding the effects of our actions and making conscious choices. It's about planting the seeds for the life we want to live.

Karma is an ethical compass for your life.

Imagine you're in a boat in the middle of the ocean. You have no map, no GPS, and no idea which way to go. You're lost, right? But then, you remember you have a compass. Suddenly, you have a direction. You know where north is, and you can navigate your way home.

That's what Karma can be for your life. It's not about fear of punishment or anticipation of reward. It's about having a sense of direction. It's about knowing that your actions matter and can guide you toward a life of peace, compassion, and understanding.

There were times when I felt like I was rowing against the current. It wasn't easy, but I kept going. I kept following my ethical compass. And you know what? It led me to a place of peace and understanding. It led me home.

So, how can you use Karma as an ethical compass in your life? It starts with mindfulness. Pay attention to your actions and their effects. Are they causing harm or promoting peace? Are they driven by selfish desires or compassionate intentions?

Try this exercise:

- For the next week, try to be mindful of your actions.

- At the end of each day, write down one action that you're proud of and one action that you think you could improve.

- Reflect on these actions and their effects.

- This simple exercise can help you start using Karma as an ethical compass in your life.

Remember, Karma is not a judge. It's a guide. It's a compass that can help you navigate the ocean of life.

Karma and Rebirth

Rebirth in Buddhism isn't about coming back as a different creature in your next life. It's not a literal reincarnation. Instead, it's about the continuation of consciousness. Picture it like a flame passing from one candle to another. The flame is the same, but the candles are different.

Karma and rebirth are two sides of the same coin. They're interconnected. The actions we take in this life (our Karma) influence the nature of our consciousness in the next (our rebirth).

"Each morning we are born again. What we do today matters most." - Buddha. Isn't that a fascinating way to kickstart our day? Think about it for a moment. You and I, we're continually being reborn, one moment at a time, one day at a time. In the grand scheme of things, it's what we choose to do today that shapes our tomorrow.

That's Karma for you, and as you would've guessed, it's tightly intertwined with rebirth. Now, before you get visions of being reincarnated as a grasshopper or a raccoon, let's delve a bit deeper into these concepts.

Let's talk about Karma first, the engine of cause and effect that drives our existence according to Buddhist philosophy. Don't you find it amusing that Karma has become such a pop-culture buzzword? It's almost like Karma has its own marketing team! But its popularity also comes with a suitcase full of misconceptions. So, let's unpack that suitcase and demystify Karma.

Karma, in its essence, is a fundamental law of the universe. It states that our actions, be they physical, verbal, or mental, leave an imprint on our mind that will inevitably ripen into experience when the conditions are right.

Imagine Karma as the most sophisticated 4D printer ever. You feed it with blueprints of your actions and thoughts, and it prints out corresponding experiences for you. Feed it with good, wholesome stuff, and voila! You get happy, positive experiences. Feed it with not-so-good stuff... well, you know what happens. It's like the old computer programming adage, *"Garbage in, garbage out."* Only that with Karma, it's more like *"good in, good out"* and *"bad in, bad out."*

That brings us to the second part of our discussion, rebirth. Now, it's easy to view rebirth as a kind of divine recycling program, where we get a new life form based on our past actions. But Buddhism looks at rebirth from a more nuanced perspective. It's not a simple matter of taking a new birth after death. It's about the continuous cycle of birth, death, and rebirth.

Every moment, every day, we're going through this cycle. We take actions, we face the consequences, and then we're reborn into the next moment, carrying with us the baggage of our past. It's an ongoing process, like the unending cycle of seasons or the relentless waves of the sea.

Here's another exercise for you:

Try to spend a day observing your actions and thoughts, and how they impact your mood, your interactions, and your experiences. Don't judge or change anything, just observe. You might be surprised at the insights you gain about your own cycle of karma and rebirth.

Now, this might all sound heavy and a bit overwhelming. But here's the silver lining. Buddhists believe that we have the power to change our Karma, and by doing so, change our experience of rebirth, moment by moment, day by day.

The Tibetan Book of the Dead: a classic of Buddhist wisdom on death and dying

The Tibetan Book of the Dead, or *Bardo Thodol*, is a guide for the journey after death, but it's also a guide for the journey of life. It's about understanding the impermanence of life, the cycle of death and rebirth, and the liberation that can be found in this understanding.

Now, I can almost hear you thinking, *"This sounds a bit heavy for my morning coffee reading."* And you're right. It's not light reading. But it's incredibly enlightening (pun intended).

The Tibetan Book of the Dead teaches us that death is not an end, but a transition. It's a continuation of the journey. This understanding can help us live our lives more fully, knowing that every moment is precious and fleeting.

So, how can you apply this wisdom in your life? Start by reflecting on the impermanence of life. Consider how this understanding might change your perspective on your daily experiences.

We all know about death, that inevitable truth that visits each one of us eventually. Still, death is often a taboo, a fearful topic tucked away in the back of our minds like an unwelcome guest. However, in Buddhism, death is a milestone, a transitional phase, a journey in itself. This notion resonates perfectly with the ancient Buddhist scripture known as The Tibetan Book of the Dead. Today, we will journey through its wisdom.

Imagine you're hiking on a familiar trail. You've been there countless times, and you know the turns, dips, and elevations.

But this time, you come across a previously unseen fork in the path. Two paths beckon, each with its unique landscape and intrigue. The first one is a well-trodden route, comfortable but monotonous. The other, is a less trodden path, mysterious and filled with unknown wonders.

This scenario is a metaphor for life and death. The known trail represents life, the mysterious one symbolizes death. The Tibetan Book of the Dead introduces us to this unknown trail, illustrating the journey beyond the physical world.

A profoundly transformative piece, the Tibetan Book of the Dead takes us into the *"bardos,"* intermediate stages between life, death, and rebirth. It offers an extraordinary perspective on the cyclical nature of existence, guiding the deceased and their loved ones through the process of death and beyond.

Here's a simple exercise to try:

- Jot down what death means to you.

- Your thoughts, feelings, fears, or curiosities.

This simple exercise can serve as a mirror, reflecting your understanding and relationship with this inevitable transition.

Many people shy away from such truths, afraid they might unravel existential crises or fear of mortality. But let me assure you, the Tibetan Book of the Dead is less about inciting fear and more about providing a roadmap to navigate through death with grace, understanding, and peace.

Table: Key concepts from the Tibetan Book of the Dead

CONCEPT	BRIEF DESCRIPTION
Bardos	Intermediate stages between life, death, and rebirth
Samsara	The cycle of birth, death, and rebirth
Karma	Law of cause and effect, influencing our current life and future lives
Dharmata	The intrinsic nature of reality

Let's play a game of imagination. Suppose you're on a cosmic voyage, not unlike an astronaut journeying into the unfathomable abyss of space. But this voyage is inward, delving into the deepest corridors of your consciousness, where life meets death and rebirth. The Tibetan Book of the Dead is your cosmic GPS, your spiritual compass, guiding you through the mysterious terrain of existence and non-existence.

It's important to mention that you don't need to follow the Buddhist path to derive value from this spiritual classic. Whether you're an ardent spiritual seeker, a curious skeptic, or a weary soul looking for solace, this timeless wisdom can illuminate your path and reshape your understanding of life and death.

To close, let's consider a quote from the Buddha: *"Even death is not to be feared by one who has lived wisely."* So, let's live wisely, embracing every breath with mindfulness, love, and compassion. And when death comes knocking at our door, let's greet it with the grace, peace, and understanding nurtured by the timeless wisdom of the Tibetan Book of the Dead.

Task List:

- Revisit your thoughts on death (from the exercise).

- Read a passage or chapter from the Tibetan Book of the Dead.

- Reflect on how your understanding of death might have changed.

Chapter Ten

THE THREE SCHOOLS OF BUDDHISM

"Change is never painful, only resistance to change is painful" - Buddha

Let's dig into our journey of understanding Buddhism today by considering how the spread and development of this philosophy occurred after Lord Buddha's death. Imagine the compassionate teachings of Lord Buddha, rippling out from the humble heartland of India, reaching far corners of the world and embracing different cultures, traditions, and ways of life. Just as water in a river must flow, so too did Buddhism evolve, reminding us of Buddha's essential teaching, *"Everything is subject to change."*

Theravāda or the School of the Elders

Around 250 BC, we see the emergence of *Theravāda* or the School of the Elders. The most orthodox form of Buddhism, *Theravāda* found its adherents mostly in Southeast Asia, particularly Sri Lanka (where it spread first, from India), Thailand, and Myanmar. Picture a serene temple tucked in a lush Sri Lankan jungle, monks clad in saffron robes chanting early in the morning as the day breaks, their teachings seeping into the very soil of the land. The contemporary *Vipassana* movement, and indeed, the mindfulness craze here in the West, finds its roots within *Theravāda* Buddhism. Isn't it astonishing that these teachings from over two millennia ago still resonate with us today?

Mahāyāna, the Great Vehicle

Fast forward to the 1st century BC, and the stage is set for *Mahāyāna*, the Great Vehicle, to make its grand entrance. With followers predominantly found in China, Japan, and Korea, Mahāyāna emerged with its unique characteristics. Imagine the Zen gardens of Japan or the grandiose halls of a Chinese temple filled with a profound, echoey silence. Zen and Pure Land are two schools of thought that this tradition birthed, reminding us of the diversity within Buddhism itself.

Vajrayāna, the Diamond Vehicle

Enter the 5th century AD, and we witness the birth of *Vajrayāna*, the Diamond Vehicle, which is a sparkly offshoot of *Mahāyāna*. If you were to visit Tibet around the 7th century AD, you'd see a variant of this school flourishing, known as Tibetan Buddhism. Imagine the melodic hum of mantras echoing across the rugged landscape of the Himalayas, the fluttering prayer flags, and the vibrant *thangka* paintings - a vivid testament to Buddhism's evolution.

So, as we dive deeper into the rich waters of Buddhism, it's crucial to remember that despite its different schools, the core remains consistent. The fundamentals have always been the same - promoting loving-kindness, compassion, wisdom, and peace. This is where the beauty of Buddhism lies. Each school is like a different colored thread, weaving together a stunning tapestry that depicts the wisdom of Lord Buddha.

Chapter Eleven

FINDING BALANCE IN LIFE

"Only a man himself can be a master of himself: who else outside could be his master? When the Master and servant are one, then there is true help and self possession."
- Buddha

The Importance of Balance

Have you ever tried walking on a tightrope? No? Don't worry, neither have I! The very thought of placing one foot in front of the other on a slim, tensioned piece of cord, all while swaying precariously above the ground, makes my stomach do somersaults. Yet, isn't it interesting how life often feels like this delicate balancing act?

Before we dive into the deep sea of wisdom, let's get into our metaphorical diving suits and start with a little mental exercise. Close your eyes for a moment. Imagine your life is a giant scale. On one side of the scale, you have work, obligations, and demands; on the other side, you have rest, relaxation, and joy. Now, think about it, how balanced is this scale? Is it leaning more towards one side? Are you giving more weight to work and obligations at the expense of your well-being? Or is it surprisingly balanced?

Did your metaphorical scale just topple over? If so, don't worry. This is where the essence of Buddhism sweeps in like a calming breeze, whispering the secrets of achieving that elusive balance.

When we speak of balance in Buddhism, we're not referring to that perfect poise and grace of a tightrope walker, but to a balance that stems from inner peace, understanding, and compassion - a balance that helps in reducing stress, anxiety, and the sense of unease that accompanies an unbalanced life.

Buddhism taught me the profound truth that balance is not something to be attained; it's something to be discovered within oneself. It's the harmony between our mind and body, between our desires and contentment, and most importantly, between our struggles and our peace.

This understanding of balance doesn't come overnight. It's a process, much like learning to walk on a tightrope, except without the fear of falling! It requires practicing mindfulness and meditation - the two pillars of Buddhism that help cultivate awareness, acceptance, and tranquility.

If you are grappling with the tumultuous waves of life, remember, it's okay if you stumble while trying to find your balance. That's part of the journey. But imagine this: being able to stand amidst the chaos with a serene smile, knowing that you have found your balance, your peace. That's the power of Buddhism. That's the power of balance.

Balancing Work and Personal Life

Perhaps you find yourself in a similar boat right now, juggling responsibilities and trying to keep everything afloat. But remember, amidst this storm, there is calm waiting to be found.

Picture this scenario: You're on a seesaw, the kind you might have enjoyed in your childhood. On one end, you have your work — deadlines, projects, responsibilities. On the other, you have your personal life — hobbies, relationships, self-care. The goal isn't to let one side hit the ground while the other soars high. The goal is to keep them at equilibrium, suspended in mid-air, enjoying the view.

So, how can we use the teachings of Buddhism to strike a balance between work and personal life?

Firstly, let's start with mindfulness. Mindfulness, simply put, is being fully present in the moment. When you're at work, be at work. When you're at home, be at home. Avoid thinking about your pending presentation during your son's soccer match. Similarly, don't worry about your dishwasher at home when you're in a meeting at work. Be fully present wherever you are. Easier said than done, right? Don't worry; it gets easier with practice.

To help you with this, let's do a simple exercise:

- Grab a piece of paper and a pen.

- Draw a line down the center, creating two columns. Label one as 'Work' and the other as 'Personal.'

- In the 'Work' column, list down all your key work responsibilities and tasks.

- In the 'Personal' column, write down the things that matter most to you outside of work, like spending time with family, practicing a hobby, exercising, etc.

- Now, for the next week, consciously try to be present when doing the tasks from both these columns.

This exercise will not only help you be mindful but also visualize how you are dividing your time and energy.

Secondly, remember to cultivate compassion — for others and, most importantly, for yourself. It's okay to not get everything right all the time. You're not a robot; you're a beautifully complex human being capable of extraordinary things but also susceptible to exhaustion. Don't be too hard on yourself. After all, the core of Buddhism teaches us to have loving-kindness towards all beings, including ourselves.

Thirdly, find time for meditation. Even a few minutes each day can have a significant impact. It will help you clear your mind, reduce stress, and regain focus. Trust me, it's not 'new age nonsense.' It's a practice as ancient as time itself and as beneficial as any medicine.

Lastly, accept the impermanence of everything. Projects will come and go, deadlines will pass, and your daily to-do list will eventually be cleared. Don't lose yourself in the fleeting demands of work and forget to live. Remember, life itself is transient.

Remember that quote from Buddha, "*Your work is to discover your world and then with all your heart give yourself to it.*" Your world isn't solely composed of work. It also includes you, your loved ones, your passions, and your tranquility. Discover it all, and balance will find its way to you.

The Role of Spiritual Practice in Achieving Balance

Whoosh!

Did you hear that?

That was the sound of stress, like a gust of wind, whizzing past you.

Surprised?

Ah, the magic of spiritual practice! Oh, but wait, I'm getting ahead of myself, aren't I? Let's slow down and return to the here and now, a concept central to Buddhism, after all.

Now, don't be put off by the term 'spirituality.' It's not a nebulous term reserved for monks or yogis sitting on top of distant mountains. Spirituality is simply about finding your inner peace and wisdom, your true essence. And it has a profound role in achieving balance in your life.

Picture your life as a grand orchestra. There are the booming drums of your professional commitments, the shrill violin of societal expectations, the constant rhythm of daily chores, and so on. But where's the conductor? Who's ensuring that these disparate sounds come together to create a symphony and not a cacophony? That's where spirituality steps in. It is the conductor of your life's orchestra, giving you the wisdom to strike a balance.

Cultivating Balance Through Mindfulness

In our frantic quest for achievement, we often forget to pause, to breathe, to feel. We forget that being human is not just about doing but also about simply being. We forget to balance our lives. That's where mindfulness and the teachings of Buddhism can bring a profound shift.

Alright, now that I've set the stage, let's talk about how we can cultivate balance through mindfulness.

Mindfulness is often misunderstood as merely a technique to quiet the mind. However, it's more than that. At its core, it's about being completely present in each moment, fully experiencing life as it happens. When we practice mindfulness, we practice the art of living itself. But how does this bring balance to our lives, you ask? Let's think about a tightrope walker. For them, balance is not a static state but a dynamic process. They need to be fully aware of each step, of the subtle shifts in their body, of the sway of the rope beneath them. That's precisely what mindfulness does for us. It allows us to tune in to the present moment, to the subtle shifts within us and around us. This conscious awareness can help us adjust and realign ourselves whenever we start to sway from our center.

Consider this a sort of exercise or homework, if you will. Over the next week, try to spend five minutes each day simply being present. This could mean truly savoring your morning coffee instead of gulping it down while answering emails. It could mean really listening to a piece of music, feeling the rhythm and the emotions it evokes. Or it could mean watching a sunset without reaching for your phone to capture it. Give this practice a try and see how it affects your overall sense of balance.

Now, here's where Buddhism enters the picture. Buddhism teaches us the concept of the Middle Way, a path of balance that avoids extremes. This concept applies not only to our actions but also to our thoughts and emotions. For instance, instead of getting swept away by anger or anxiety, we learn to observe these emotions without judgment, thereby preventing them from throwing us off balance.

By blending mindfulness with the teachings of Buddhism, we can cultivate a sense of balance that permeates every aspect of our lives. From our mental and emotional state to our relationships and work-life balance, everything starts to fall into a harmonious rhythm.

There's a phrase in Buddhism, *"Sati Sampajanna,"* which loosely translates to "Mindfulness and Clear Comprehension." It suggests a balanced way of living that is aware, understanding, and kind. It's like walking on that tightrope with grace and ease, perfectly balanced, fully aware, completely in the moment.

Strategies for Maintaining Balance

Balance - it's a word we hear often, isn't it? We strive for it in our diets, our work, and our personal life, even in our yoga poses. But what about our minds? Our emotions? Our spiritual selves?

Does that sound familiar? If so, you're not alone. It's a common experience in today's fast-paced, high-pressure world. But it doesn't have to be this way.

The Buddhist concept called the Middle Way is a path of moderation, a path that avoids extremes and seeks balance in all things. It's not about swinging from one extreme to another, but about finding a steady, stable center. And it's not just a philosophical concept, but a practical guide for living a balanced, calm life.

So, how do we find this balance? Here are some strategies that will help.

Mindfulness and Meditation

Practice being fully present and engaged with whatever you're doing, whether it's washing the dishes, walking in the park, or sitting in a meeting.

Meditation, on the other hand, is a more formal practice where you set aside time to focus your mind and cultivate mindfulness. It's like a workout for your mind, strengthening your ability to stay present and focused.

Together, mindfulness and meditation can help you find balance by reducing stress, improving mental clarity, and promoting emotional well-being. They can help you stay centered amidst the chaos of daily life and respond to challenges with calmness and clarity.

Self-care

In our busy lives, it's easy to neglect our own needs. But self-care is not a luxury, it's a necessity. It's about taking care of your physical, emotional, and spiritual well-being. This can include things like eating a healthy diet, getting regular exercise, getting enough sleep, and taking time for relaxation and leisure activities.

But it's also about setting boundaries and saying no when necessary. It's about recognizing your limits and not overextending yourself. It's about treating yourself with kindness and compassion, just as you would treat a loved one.

Connection with Others

We are social creatures, and we need connection with others to thrive. This can include spending time with family and friends, participating in social activities, or volunteering in your community.

But it's not just about quantity, but quality of connection. It's about having meaningful, supportive relationships where you feel seen, heard, and valued. It's about being there for others, but also allowing others to be there for you.

Spiritual Practice

Whatever your spiritual beliefs or practices, they can provide a sense of purpose, meaning, and connection that can anchor you in the midst of life's storms.

Whether it's prayer, meditation, reading spiritual texts, attending religious services, or simply spending time in nature, spiritual practice can help you connect with something larger than yourself and remind you of the bigger picture.

Exercise: Finding Your Balance

- Take a moment to reflect on your own life. How balanced does it feel? Are there areas where you're leaning too far in one direction, and need to pull back? Are there areas where you're neglecting your needs?

- Take a piece of paper and draw a large circle on it. Divide the circle into four quadrants and label them: Mindfulness and Meditation, Self-Care, Connection with Others, and Spiritual Practice.

- In each quadrant, jot down what you're currently doing in that area and rate your level of satisfaction from 1-10.

- Then, brainstorm some ways you could improve your balance in that area.

Remember, balance is not a destination, but a journey. It's not about achieving perfection, but about making small, consistent adjustments to keep yourself on track.

Chapter Twelve

BUDDHISM AND THE ENVIRONMENT

"Even as on a heap of rubbish thrown away by the side of the road, a lotus flower may grow and blossom with its pure perfume giving joy to the soul, in the same way among the blind multitudes shines pure the light of wisdom of the student who follows the Buddha, the One who is truly awake." - Buddha

The Buddhist Perspective on Environmentalism

"Every blade of grass has its angel that bends over it and whispers, 'grow, grow.'" This quote from the Talmud, a central text of Rabbinic Judaism, may not be directly related to Buddhism, but it beautifully encapsulates the essence of what I'm about to share with you. It's about our relationship with the environment, seen through the lens of Buddhist philosophy.

Imagine, if you will, a quiet morning. The sun is just beginning to peek over the horizon, casting a warm, golden light over a lush, verdant landscape. Dewdrops sparkle on the leaves, and the air is filled with the sweet scent of blooming flowers. You take a deep breath, and for a moment, you feel a profound sense of peace. This is the beauty of nature that Buddhism teaches us to cherish and protect.

Buddhism, at its core, is about understanding the interconnectedness of all things. It teaches us that we are not separate entities, but rather, we are part of a vast, intricate web of life. This understanding extends to our relationship with the environment. We are not mere observers or exploiters of nature; we are part of it, and what we do to it, we do to ourselves.

In Buddhism, there's a concept known as "dependent origination," which posits that all phenomena arise in dependence upon multiple causes and conditions. Nothing exists as a solitary, independent entity. This principle applies to our environment as well. The air we breathe, the water we drink, the food we eat - all are products of a complex ecological system that we are intrinsically a part of.

Now, let's take a moment to reflect on our current environmental crisis. Climate change, deforestation, and pollution - these are not just abstract concepts. They are real, tangible issues that affect us all. And they are, in large part, the result of our collective actions.

But here's the good news: just as our actions have contributed to these problems, so too can they be part of the solution. And this is where the Buddhist perspective on environmentalism comes into play.

Buddhism teaches us to live mindfully and to be fully present in each moment. When we apply this principle to our interaction with the environment, we begin to see the impact of our actions. We start to understand that every choice we make - from the products we buy to the way we dispose of our waste - has an effect on our planet.

So, what can we do? How can we, as individuals, make a difference? Here are a few suggestions:

- Practice mindful consumption: Be aware of what you're buying and where it comes from. Try to choose products that are environmentally friendly and ethically produced.

- Reduce, reuse, recycle: These three R's are the cornerstone of sustainable living. Try to minimize waste, repurpose items when possible, and recycle what you can't reuse.

- Plant a tree: Trees are the lungs of our planet. They absorb carbon dioxide and release oxygen, helping to combat climate change. Plus, they provide habitat for countless species of animals and insects.

- Support environmental organizations: There are many groups out there doing fantastic work to protect our environment. Consider donating to them or volunteering your time.

- Spread the word: Talk to your friends, family, and colleagues about the importance of environmental conservation. The more people are aware of the issue, the more we can do to address it.

Remember, every action counts, no matter how small it may seem. As the Buddha once said, *"Thousands of candles can be lighted from a single candle, and the life of the single candle will not be shortened. Happiness never decreases by being shared."* Similarly, our collective efforts to protect the environment will not diminish our individual lives but instead enrich them.

Here's an exercise that I'd like to share with you:

The next time you're outside, take a moment to really observe your surroundings. Feel the sun on your skin, listen to the birds singing, and smell the fresh air. Then, close your eyes and imagine what it would be like if all of this were gone. It's a sobering thought, isn't it?

This exercise is not meant to scare you, but rather to inspire you. It's a reminder of what's at stake - and what we stand to gain by embracing a more sustainable way of living. After all, in protecting the environment, we're not just preserving the beauty of nature. We're also safeguarding our own well-being and that of future generations.

The Principles of Interdependence

Once upon a time, in a bustling city, there was a man named John. John was a successful businessman, always on the move, and always busy. He was the epitome of the modern man, constantly juggling multiple responsibilities and demands. But one day, John found himself standing in the middle of a crowded street, feeling utterly alone. He felt disconnected as if he was an island in the middle of a vast ocean. This feeling of isolation, of disconnection, was the catalyst that led John to explore the principles of interdependence.

Now, you might be wondering, *"What on earth is interdependence?"* Let me explain. Interdependence is a fundamental principle in Buddhism. It's the idea that everything in the universe is interconnected, that we are all part of a vast, intricate web of relationships. Nothing exists in isolation. Everything affects everything else.

Think of it like this: imagine you're holding a beautiful, ripe apple in your hand. That apple didn't just magically appear. It's the result of countless factors working together - the seed, the soil, the sun, the rain, the farmer who tended the tree, the truck driver who transported the fruit to the market, and so on. This is interdependence in action.

Understanding this principle can have profound implications for our lives. It can help us realize that our actions have consequences, and that what we do matters. It can foster a sense of responsibility, compassion, and empathy. It can help us see that we are not alone, that we are part of something bigger than ourselves.

Let's go back to our friend John. After his moment of realization on that crowded street, John started to see the world differently. He began to understand that his actions had an impact on the people around him. He realized that his success was not just the result of his own efforts, but also the result of the support and cooperation of countless others. This understanding transformed John's life. He became more compassionate, more considerate, more connected.

Now, I'm not saying that understanding the principle of interdependence will magically solve all your problems. But it can provide a new perspective, a new way of seeing the world. It can help you realize that you are not alone, that your actions matter, and that you are part of a vast, interconnected web of life.

So, how can you apply this principle in your own life? Here are a few suggestions:

- Practice mindfulness: Pay attention to the present moment. Notice the interconnections in your life. Appreciate the people, the circumstances, and the natural forces that make your life possible.

- Cultivate gratitude: Take a moment each day to express gratitude for the people and circumstances that support your life. This can help you feel more connected and less isolated.

- Act with compassion: Recognize that your actions have an impact on others. Try to act in ways that promote harmony and well-being.

- Reflect on interdependence: Take some time each day to reflect on the principle of interdependence. This can help you deepen your understanding and appreciation of this principle.

Mindful Consumption

"Life is like a sandwich - the more you add to it, the better it becomes." Now, I'm not sure who said that, but I'm pretty sure they weren't talking about adding more stress, anxiety, or unhealthy habits to our lives. They were probably thinking more along the lines of joy, love, and, of course, mindful consumption.

Mindful consumption – you may be thinking *"What does this actually mean?"* Well, allow me to shed some light on the matter. It's not about counting calories or obsessively checking the labels on your food, although those can be part of it. Mindful consumption is about much more than just what we eat or drink.

It's about everything we take into our bodies, our minds, and our hearts.

Mindful consumption is about being fully present and aware of what we're taking in, whether it's food, information, or emotions. It's about making conscious choices that nourish us and support our well-being, rather than deplete us.

Let's start with food, as it's something that's part of all our lives. Mindful consumption means really paying attention to what we eat, savoring each bite, and appreciating the nourishment it provides. It's about choosing foods that are healthy and beneficial for our bodies, rather than just reaching for the nearest snack when we're hungry or stressed.

But it doesn't stop at food. What about the information we consume? In this digital age, we're constantly bombarded with news, social media updates, emails, and more. Mindful consumption means being selective about the information we take in, focusing on what's truly beneficial, and avoiding the negativity and noise that can overwhelm us.

And then there's emotional consumption. This might be a new concept for you. But think about it - we often take on the emotions and energy of the people and environments around us. Mindful consumption in this context means being aware of this and choosing to surround ourselves with positive influences that uplift us rather than bring us down.

Now, I know this might sound like a lot to take in. But don't worry, I'm not suggesting you overhaul your entire life overnight. Like any journey, it starts with a single step. And the first step towards mindful consumption is simply awareness.

So, here's a little exercise for you:

Over the next week, try to pay attention to what you're consuming - food, information, emotions - and note down how it makes you feel. You might be surprised at what you discover.

Imagine this: You're at a bustling farmers market on a sunny Saturday morning. The air is filled with the aroma of fresh produce, the chatter of excited shoppers, and the occasional laughter of children running around. You're standing in front of a stall that sells apples. There are so many varieties - some you've never even heard of before. You pick up a shiny, red apple and take a moment to appreciate its beauty. You feel its weight in your hand, observe its color, and take a deep breath to smell its freshness. You're not just buying an apple; you're experiencing it.

Mindful consumption encompasses everything we take in - the books we read, the music we listen to, the conversations we have, the social media posts we scroll through, and yes, even the air we breathe. It's about being present and aware of what we're consuming and how it affects us.

Now, you might be thinking, *"That sounds great, but I'm already juggling a million things. How am I supposed to add one more thing to my plate?"* Well, let me assure you, mindful consumption is not another chore to tick off your to-do list. It's a way of life that can actually make your life simpler and more meaningful.

Let's take a moment to understand why mindful consumption is so important. In our fast-paced, consumer-driven society, we're constantly bombarded with information, choices, and demands. We're often on autopilot, mindlessly consuming without really thinking about what we're taking in or why. This can lead to stress, anxiety, and a feeling of being overwhelmed. It can also disconnect us from our true selves and what really matters to us.

Mindful consumption, on the other hand, encourages us to slow down and make conscious choices. It helps us to tune in to our needs and desires, and to make decisions that align with our values and enhance our well-being. It allows us to savor the joy of simple pleasures and cultivate gratitude for the abundance in our lives.

So, how can you practice mindful consumption? Here are a few suggestions:

- Be present: Whether you're eating a meal, reading a book, or scrolling through social media, try to be fully present. Pay attention to your senses and your emotions.

Notice how what you're consuming makes you feel.

- Make conscious choices: Before you consume something, ask yourself: Do I really need this? Does it add value to my life? Does it align with my values?

- Savor the moment: Take the time to truly enjoy what you're consuming. Savor the flavors of your food, the beauty of a sunset, the melody of a song.

- Cultivate gratitude: Take a moment each day to appreciate the abundance in your life. Express gratitude for the food you eat, the air you breathe, the people you love.

- Practice moderation: Too much of a good thing can be harmful. Practice moderation in all aspects of consumption.

Remember, mindful consumption is not about perfection. It's about progress. It's about making small, conscious choices each day that add up to significant changes over time. It's about finding joy in the journey, not just the destination.

Let's take a walk down memory lane, shall we? Remember when we were kids, and the world was a giant playground? We would run around, exploring every nook and cranny, tasting every new fruit, touching every new texture, and smelling every new scent. We were mindful consumers, taking in the world one sense at a time. But as we grew older, we started to lose that mindfulness. We started to consume mindlessly, be it food, media, or even relationships. It's time to go back to our childlike nature where mindful consumption is concerned and rediscover the joys it can bring to our life!

Chapter Thirteen

APPLYING BUDDHIST TEACHINGS IN TODAY'S WORLD

"Joy is born in one who has delight, the body of one who has joy is calmed, one whose body is calmed feels ease, and the mind of one who is at ease is contemplative." - Buddha

Buddhism in the Digital Age

"Life moves pretty fast. If you don't stop and look around once in a while, you could miss it." - 'Ferris Bueller's Day Off'.

Isn't it fascinating how a quote from a 1986 teen comedy movie can encapsulate the essence of Buddhism? It's as if Ferris Bueller was a modern-day, high school Buddha in a leather jacket, teaching us the importance of mindfulness in the midst of our fast-paced, digital lives.

Now, let's dive into the heart of the matter - Buddhism in the digital age.

As we flicker our thumbs and tap our screens, we've woven a reality where life unfurls in 140-character tweets, filtered snapshots, and viral TikTok dances. We're living in the digital age, a period of unparalleled connectivity and information access, yet it's an era marked by a unique kind of distraction and disconnect. Amid the cacophony of digital noise, how can we find peace, purpose, and mindfulness? Here is where Buddhism, an ancient philosophy with timeless wisdom, steps onto our modern, pixelated stage.

Buddhism, in its serene simplicity, offers a refuge from our hyperactive, digitally-driven world. It invites us to unplug, if only momentarily, from the constant buzz of notifications and the relentless pursuit of likes and followers. It's a gentle reminder to close our apps, put our devices away, and simply breathe. It tells us that we don't always have to be 'online' to truly live.

In the heart of Buddhism lies mindfulness - a profound awareness and acceptance of the present moment, devoid of judgment. It's about being truly present, not simply 'logged in.' In this era where multi-tasking is celebrated and our attention is split among a myriad of digital distractions, mindfulness is more crucial than ever.

But let's not view the digital age as a foe to our spiritual journey. Technology, like any tool, is as beneficial or detrimental as we allow it to be. And believe it or not, our digitized world has the potential to serve as a powerful ally on our path to enlightenment.

Take the proliferation of meditation apps, online Buddhist communities, and digital Dharma teachings. These tools make the teachings of Buddhism accessible to anyone with an internet connection. You can now join a meditation group half a world away, attend Dharma talks from renowned Buddhist monks, or engage in philosophical discussions in virtual Buddhist forums. In many ways, the digital age has democratized access to Buddhist teachings, tearing down geographical and cultural barriers.

Digital platforms also allow us to build *Sanghas* - communities of practitioners - that transcend physical boundaries. In these spaces, support, understanding, and wisdom flow freely, helping us navigate our spiritual path. Through technology, we're capable of forging connections that enrich our understanding of Buddhism, and ourselves.

Let's remember, though, that the merging of Buddhism and the digital age is a delicate paradox that needs careful navigation, like a Zen *koan*. A *koan* is a conundrum with no obvious solution, a special type of meditation offered by Zen practice. It's our responsibility to strike a balance - to leverage digital resources to enhance our understanding and practice of Buddhism, while not losing ourselves in the virtual abyss.

But here's the good news - Buddhism, with its timeless wisdom, offers a way out of this digital maze. It teaches us to slow down, be present, and cultivate mindfulness, even amidst the chaos of the digital world.

Think of mindfulness as your personal 'pause' button in the middle of a hectic day. It's about being fully present in the moment, not lost in your thoughts, your worries about the future, or your regrets about the past. It's about fully experiencing the now - the taste of your coffee, the feel of the wind against your skin, the sound of your breath.

Now, you might be wondering, *"How do I practice mindfulness in the digital age? Do I have to give up my smartphone and move to a monastery in the Himalayas?"*

Well, the answer is no. You don't have to give up your digital devices or your lifestyle. Instead, you can learn to use them mindfully.

Here's a simple exercise to get you started:

- The next time you pick up your smartphone, pause for a moment. Take a deep breath.

- As you unlock your phone, pay attention to the sensation of your fingers touching the screen.

- As you scroll through your apps or your social media feed, stay aware of your thoughts and emotions. Are you feeling anxious? Excited? Bored?

- Every once in a while, take a break. Put down your phone, close your eyes, and take a few deep breaths.

This is just a simple example, but it's a start. The key is to bring this kind of awareness to all aspects of your digital life, whether you're sending an email, watching a video, or participating in a virtual meeting.

In the end, Buddhism in the digital age is not about rejecting technology, but about using it in a way that supports our well-being, rather than detracts from it. It's about finding balance, calm, and compassion in the midst of our digital lives.

So, the next time you find yourself mindlessly scrolling through your social media feed, remember Ferris Bueller's wise words. Life moves pretty fast. Don't forget to stop and look around once in a while. After all, the present moment is all we really have.

And who knows? You might just find a bit of enlightenment in between your tweets and TikTok's.

The Challenges of Modern Life

"Life is what happens to us while we are making other plans." - Allen Saunders. Isn't it funny how we often find ourselves caught in the whirlwind of modern life, spinning like a top, barely keeping our balance? We're constantly juggling work, family, social obligations, and personal interests, all while trying to squeeze in a few precious moments of peace and quiet. It's like we're on a never-ending treadmill, always running but never really getting anywhere.

So, how do you do this? How do you integrate these ancient principles into your modern life? Well, that's what this book is all about. It's a guide, a roadmap, a blueprint for finding balance, peace, and happiness in the midst of the chaos and stress of modern life.

But before we dive into the how, let's take a moment to understand the why. Why are we so stressed and anxious in the first place? What is it about modern life that makes us feel like we're constantly running on a treadmill, always busy but never really getting anywhere?

Here's an exercise for you to delve deeper into the why:

- Take a moment to think about your typical day.

- What does it look like?

- How do you feel? Are you constantly rushing from one task to another, always feeling like you're behind, never really able to relax and enjoy the moment?

- Do you feel like you're constantly juggling multiple demands, always trying to please everyone but never really pleasing yourself?

The Relevance of Buddhist Teachings Today

Let's take a moment to imagine ourselves in a bustling city. The honking of cars, the rush of people, the towering skyscrapers, the constant hum of life. It's exhilarating, isn't it? But also, quite exhausting. Now, let's take a deep breath and transport ourselves to a serene mountaintop, the air crisp and fresh, the silence only broken by the occasional chirping of birds. Quite a contrast, isn't it? This is the contrast I want to draw between our modern, hectic lives and the calm, peaceful teachings of Buddhism.

You see, the teachings of Buddhism are like that serene mountaintop. They offer a refuge from the chaos of our daily lives, a sanctuary where we can find peace and tranquility. But more than just a refuge, they provide us with a roadmap, a guide to navigating the tumultuous seas of life with grace and equanimity.

Now, you might be thinking, "*That sounds wonderful, but how is this ancient philosophy relevant to my life today? I have bills to pay, a job to keep, and a family to take care of. I don't have time for mountaintops and tranquility.*" And that is true. Life is demanding. But that's precisely why the teachings of Buddhism are more relevant today than ever before.

Let's take the concept of mindfulness, for instance. In a world where we're constantly bombarded by information and distractions, mindfulness teaches us to slow down, to be present, and to truly engage with the world around us. It's not about escaping our responsibilities, but rather about approaching them with a clear mind and a calm heart. It's about finding peace amidst the chaos, not away from it.

As our journey through the intricate maze of Buddhist philosophy continues, we now find ourselves standing at a crossroads. One path beckons us towards a historical understanding of the *Dharma*, lined with the vibrant tapestry of ancient traditions and the teachings of Siddhartha Gautama, the Buddha himself. The other invites us towards a more contemporary interpretation, paved with the digital print of our modern society.

If we choose the latter, we find ourselves faced with a daunting question - is there a place for Buddhism in our lightning-paced, technology-driven, and distraction-filled world? More to the point, what relevance do Buddhist teachings hold for us today?

The answer, perhaps surprisingly, is extraordinarily simple: immeasurable relevance.

The first thread to unravel lies in the beating heart of Buddhism - mindfulness. In an era where multi-tasking is revered and where our minds flit from one notification to another, mindfulness seems like a beacon of tranquility in a storm. It encourages us to pause, to breathe, to simply be present. It gently nudges us towards acknowledging our emotions rather than suppressing them; our stresses rather than ignoring them; and our thoughts rather than brushing them aside. It asks us not to master the art of detachment, but the gentle grace of non-attachment. It is not about being devoid of emotions, but being fully present with them. In a world plagued with stress and anxiety, the simplicity and grounding nature of mindfulness holds an invaluable remedy.

Another powerful Buddhist teaching that shines brightly in the contemporary landscape is interconnectedness. We live in a world that is paradoxically connected and disconnected at the same time. Social media and technology connect us across the globe, yet we often feel isolated and detached from our immediate surroundings and even from ourselves. Buddhism teaches us that we are deeply interconnected with one another and with the universe itself. This understanding can kindle a sense of universal responsibility and compassion, thereby fostering a greater commitment towards social justice, environmental sustainability, and global peace.

Equally relevant is the concept of impermanence, the realization that all things are transient and subject to change. In our quest for control and certainty, we often find ourselves in a state of constant anxiety. The wisdom of impermanence can help us develop resilience in the face of change and uncertainty, and inspire us to appreciate and value the fleeting moments of life.

Finally, the core Buddhist teaching of suffering and the cessation of suffering, encapsulated in the Four Noble Truths, remains profoundly relevant. Buddhism offers a pragmatic approach to understanding the nature of suffering and provides practical tools to navigate our way through it. In a world where mental health issues are escalating, this compassionate approach toward understanding suffering has the potential to catalyze profound healing and growth.

It is a testament to the timelessness of the Buddha's teachings that they resonate so profoundly with the human condition, even two and a half millennia after their initial utterance. In the cacophony of our modern world, they stand as a soft-spoken reminder of our inherent capacity for wisdom, compassion, and peace. It is not so much a question of fitting Buddhism into our modern lives, but rather allowing these teachings to guide and illuminate our journey through it.

And then there's the concept of loving-kindness. Amidst a world that often feels divided and contentious, loving-kindness encourages us to cultivate compassion and understanding, not just for others, but also for ourselves. It's a reminder that we're all interconnected, that our actions have ripple effects, and that kindness and compassion are not signs of weakness, but of strength.

But perhaps the most relevant teaching of Buddhism for our modern world is the concept of impermanence. Everything changes, nothing stays the same. This can be a hard pill to swallow, especially in a society that often equates stability with success. But recognizing the impermanence of life can also be incredibly liberating. It can free us from the fear of change and open us up to new possibilities. It can help us appreciate the present moment, knowing that it's fleeting and precious.

So, how can we integrate these teachings into our daily lives?

Well, I have a few suggestions:

- **Start with mindfulness:** Try to incorporate mindfulness into your daily routine. This could be as simple as taking a few moments each day to focus on your breath, or it could involve a more formal mindfulness meditation practice.

- **Practice loving-kindness:** Make a conscious effort to cultivate compassion and understanding in your interactions with others. This could be as simple as offering a kind word or a helping hand, or it could involve a more formal loving-kindness meditation practice.

- **Embrace impermanence:** Try to view change not as something to be feared, but as an opportunity for growth and transformation. This could involve reframing your perspective on a challenging situation, or it could involve a more formal contemplation on the nature of impermanence.

Remember, the goal is not to become a perfect Buddhist overnight, but rather to gradually integrate these teachings into your life in a way that feels authentic and meaningful to you. It's not about reaching some distant mountaintop, but about finding peace and tranquility right here, amid our everyday lives.

Now, I'd like to leave you with a little exercise:

- I want you to take a moment to reflect on one area of your life where you feel stressed or overwhelmed.

- Now, consider how the teachings of mindfulness, loving-kindness, and impermanence might help you navigate this situation.

- Write down your thoughts and revisit them whenever you need a reminder of the relevance of these timeless teachings.

In the end, the relevance of Buddhist teachings today lies in their timeless wisdom, their practical guidance, and their profound capacity to transform our lives from the inside out. They remind us that amidst the hustle and bustle of our modern lives, there is a place of peace and tranquility within each of us, waiting to be discovered. And that is a discovery worth making.

Integrating Buddhist Practices into Daily Life

Let's take your morning coffee, for example. Instead of gulping it down while scrolling through your emails, take a moment to truly experience it. Feel the warmth of the cup in your hands, inhale the rich aroma, and taste the bitterness tempered by sweetness. This simple act of mindfulness can transform a mundane task into a moment of tranquility and awareness.

But it's not just about mindfulness. It's also about compassion, loving-kindness, and understanding. Remember that annoying co-worker who never seems to stop talking? Try looking at them with compassion. Maybe they're lonely or insecure. Maybe your understanding could make their day a little better.

And what about that homeless person you pass by every day? Instead of ignoring them, offer a smile, a kind word, a drink, and some food, or if you can, a helping hand. This act of loving-kindness could mean the world to them, and it could transform your own heart in the process.

Now, I'm not saying it's easy. It requires practice, patience, and persistence. But trust me, the rewards are worth it. Imagine a life where stress and anxiety are replaced with calm and peace, where anger and resentment give way to compassion and understanding. That's the power of Buddhism.

To help you on this journey, I've included a few exercises at the end of this section. They're simple, practical, and designed to fit into your busy schedule. Give them a try, and remember, it's not about perfection. It's about progress, one mindful step at a time.

Integrating Buddhism into your daily life is like learning to dance in the rain instead of waiting for the storm to pass. It's about finding peace amidst chaos, joy amidst suffering, and light amidst darkness. It's about transforming your life, one mindful moment at a time. And trust me, once you start this journey, there's no turning back.

So, are you ready to dance in the rain?

Cultivating Mindfulness in Daily Activities

In this section, we will explore practical ways to integrate Buddhist practices into your daily life and discover the profound impact they can have on your well-being and sense of fulfillment.

Mindfulness is the cornerstone of Buddhist practice, and it can be applied to every aspect of your life. From the moment you wake up to the time you go to bed, you can infuse your activities with mindful awareness.

Engage in everyday tasks with full presence, whether it's brushing your teeth, preparing a meal, or walking in nature. By staying fully present in each moment, you can experience a deeper connection to the world around you and develop a sense of gratitude for the simple joys of life.

Practice mindful eating by savoring each bite, and being aware of the flavors, textures, and nourishment that the food provides. This can help you develop a healthier relationship with food and cultivate a greater appreciation for the nourishment it brings to your body and mind. Mindful eating has also been shown to improve digestion problems and aid in losing weight because your awareness of what you are consuming more slowly means you feel fuller sooner and you will eat less.

Bringing Compassion to Interactions

One of the core teachings of Buddhism is compassion. You

can bring this quality into your daily interactions with others, whether they are your family, friends, colleagues, or even strangers.

Cultivate empathy by actively listening to others and seeking to understand their perspectives. Show kindness and offer support when someone is going through a difficult time. Small acts of compassion can have a ripple effect, creating a more harmonious and caring environment.

Practice loving-kindness meditation, where you extend well-wishes and goodwill to yourself and others. This practice can help dissolve barriers and foster a sense of interconnectedness with all beings.

Finding Moments of Stillness and Reflection

In the midst of a busy day, it's important to carve out moments of stillness and reflection. These moments allow you to reconnect with yourself and gain clarity amidst the noise and distractions.

Set aside time for meditation, even if it's just a few minutes each day. Find a quiet space where you can sit comfortably and observe your breath or engage in a guided meditation. Meditation can help calm the mind, reduce stress, and cultivate a sense of inner peace.

Create a daily ritual for self-reflection, such as journaling or contemplative walks. Use this time to explore your thoughts, emotions, and experiences without judgment. This practice can deepen your self-awareness and provide valuable insights into your own patterns of behavior and reactions.

Embracing Impermanence and Letting Go

Buddhism teaches us that everything is impermanent and clinging to things causes suffering. By embracing the impermanence of life, we can learn to let go of attachments and find freedom in the present moment.

Reflect on the transient nature of life and the ever-changing nature of experiences. Recognize that joy and sorrow, success and failure, all come and go. By cultivating this understanding, you can navigate the ups and downs of life with greater resilience and equanimity.

Practice the art of letting go by releasing expectations and attachments. Allow things to unfold naturally without trying to control or manipulate outcomes. This practice can bring a sense of lightness and freedom, allowing you to embrace life's flow with open arms.

So, there you have it. A few simple ways to integrate Buddhist practices into your daily life. Remember, it's not about becoming a Buddhist or changing who you are. It's about finding tools to help you navigate this crazy, beautiful, chaotic thing we call life. And who knows? You might just find that peace and balance you've been searching for.

Chapter Fourteen

THE PATH TO PERSONAL GROWTH AND TRANSFORMATION

"As a solid rock is indifferent to the wind and rain, so the wise are indifferent to criticism and praise." - *Buddha*

Setting Meaningful Goals

"Where are you going?" That's a question we often neglect to ask ourselves in the midst of our busy lives. We find ourselves caught up in a whirlwind of responsibilities, obligations, and never-ending to-do lists. We ride the horse of life without truly knowing our destination. It's time to pause and reflect, to set meaningful goals that align with our deepest desires and values.

This is a classic Buddhism parable:

"The horse is galloping quickly, and it appears that the rider on the horse is going somewhere important. Another man, standing alongside the road, shouts, 'Where are you going?' and the rider replies, 'I don't know! Ask the horse!'"

In Buddhism, the concept of setting goals is not about chasing external achievements or accumulating material wealth. Instead, it's about cultivating inner transformation and finding a path toward wisdom, understanding, loving-kindness, compassion, calm, and peace. It's about discovering what truly matters to us and taking intentional steps to live in alignment with those values.

Setting meaningful goals begins with self-reflection. Take a moment to connect with your innermost self and ask, "*What is it that I truly want in life?*" Allow yourself to dream without limitations, to envision a life filled with purpose, joy, and contentment. It may be helpful to grab a pen and paper and jot down your thoughts and aspirations.

As you delve deeper into this process, you might encounter resistance or doubts. The mind often throws obstacles in our path, questioning our worthiness or the feasibility of our goals. But remember, these doubts are just thoughts - they do not define you. Acknowledge them, but don't let them hold you back.

Now, let's talk about the power of intention. Setting meaningful goals is not merely about wishful thinking; it requires clarity and intentionality. When you set an intention, you declare to yourself and the universe what you truly desire. It's like planting a seed in the fertile soil of your mind, nurturing it with focused attention and action.

Consider this: if you don't know where you want to go, any road will take you there. But if you have a clear destination in mind, every step you take becomes purposeful and meaningful. Your actions align with your aspirations, guiding you toward a life of fulfillment and inner peace.

To help you set meaningful goals, consider the following questions:

- What brings me joy and fulfilment?

- What are my core values and beliefs?

- How can I align my goals with my values?

- What steps can I take today to move closer to my desired destination?

- How can I incorporate mindfulness and meditation into my goal-setting process?

Remember, setting meaningful goals is an ongoing process. As you grow and evolve, your goals may also evolve.

The Role of Self-Awareness

"Knowing yourself is the beginning of all wisdom." - Aristotle

Have you ever paused for a moment and wondered, *"Who am I? What defines me?"* These questions often arise when we find ourselves feeling lost, overwhelmed, or disconnected from the world around us. In the pursuit of understanding ourselves and seeking inner peace, self-awareness plays a crucial role.

Self-awareness, in the context of Buddhism, goes beyond simply recognizing our physical attributes or superficial qualities. It delves deeper into exploring the nature of our mind, emotions, and thoughts. By cultivating self-awareness, we embark on a transformative journey that can lead to wisdom, compassion, and ultimately, a sense of calm and peace.

In Buddhism, self-awareness is not about self-centeredness or ego-driven pursuits. Instead, it involves developing a keen sense of observation and understanding of our own mental and emotional processes. It is through this awareness that we gain insight into the patterns, habits, and conditioning that shape our experiences.

Through the practice of meditation and mindfulness, we can cultivate self-awareness. By sitting in stillness and observing our thoughts without judgment, we start to unravel the layers of our mind. We become aware of the constant chatter, the stream of thoughts that often dominates our consciousness. As we observe these thoughts, we begin to realize that we are not our thoughts; we are the observers of our thoughts.

This realization is a powerful shift in perspective. It allows us to detach from the fluctuations of our mind and create a space for inner clarity and peace. With self-awareness, we become less reactive to external circumstances and more responsive from a place of understanding and compassion.

Self-awareness also brings to light our habitual patterns and emotional reactions. We begin to notice recurring patterns of behavior that no longer serve us. By observing these patterns, we gain the opportunity to make conscious choices and break free from the cycle of suffering. We can choose to respond with kindness and compassion rather than reacting impulsively out of anger or fear.

Moreover, self-awareness helps us cultivate a deeper connection with ourselves and others. As we develop a greater understanding of our own thoughts and emotions, we also become more attuned to the experiences of those around us. This empathy and compassion arise naturally from the recognition that we are all interconnected beings on this shared journey of life.

Practicing self-awareness is not always easy. It requires patience, persistence, and a willingness to face our own vulnerabilities and shadows. However, the rewards are immeasurable. By embracing self-awareness, we embark on a path of self-discovery and transformation. We learn to navigate life's challenges with grace and resilience. We cultivate a sense of inner peace and contentment that transcends external circumstances.

<u>Here's a simple exercise for you to try:</u>

- Take a few moments each day to sit in stillness and observe your thoughts without judgment.

- Notice the patterns and emotions that arise.

- How do they influence your actions and reactions?

By cultivating self-awareness, you can begin to create a profound shift in your relationship with yourself and the world around you.

Embracing Change and Uncertainty

"Life is a series of natural and spontaneous changes. Don't resist them; that only creates sorrow. Let reality be reality. Let things flow naturally forward in whatever way they like." - Lao Tzu

Change is an inherent part of life. From the moment we are born, we are thrust into a world that is constantly evolving and shifting. Yet, many of us find ourselves resisting change, clinging to the familiar and predictable. We fear the unknown and crave stability, even when it may not serve our best interests.

In Buddhism, there is profound wisdom in embracing change and uncertainty. It teaches us to flow with the ever-changing river of life, rather than resisting or trying to control it. This philosophy can be a source of great liberation and peace, particularly in times of turmoil or transition.

Think about a river flowing effortlessly downstream. It encounters obstacles along its path, but it adapts, changes course, and continues its journey. It doesn't hold onto the past or worry about the future. It simply flows in the present moment, fully immersed in the experience. We can learn a lot from the river's resilience and adaptability.

When we resist change, we create unnecessary suffering for ourselves. We become attached to outcomes, people, and circumstances, clinging desperately to what we know, even if it no longer serves us. This attachment leads to frustration, disappointment, and a sense of being stuck.

However, when we embrace change and uncertainty, we open ourselves up to new possibilities and growth. We learn to let go of our attachment to outcomes and surrender to the flow of life. It doesn't mean that we become passive or complacent; rather, we develop the ability to respond skillfully to whatever arises.

Practicing mindfulness and meditation can greatly support our ability to embrace change. By cultivating present-moment awareness, we become attuned to the ever-changing nature of our thoughts, emotions, and sensations. We develop the capacity to observe these experiences without judgment or resistance.

In this process, we discover a profound truth: change is inevitable, but suffering is optional. When we let go of our attachment to how things should be and accept them as they are, we find a sense of freedom and peace. We become more resilient in the face of challenges and more open to the possibilities that change brings.

Let's explore the process with a simple exercise:

- Take a moment to reflect on a recent change or uncertainty you have faced in your life.

- How did you initially react to it?

- Did you resist or embrace it?

- What were the consequences of your response?

- Now, imagine how it would feel to approach a similar situation with an open mind and heart.

- How might embracing change and uncertainty enhance your well-being and sense of inner peace?

Remember, change is an opportunity for growth and transformation. By embracing it, we can navigate the ever-changing currents of life with greater ease and grace.

Cultivating Resilience and Adaptability

"Life doesn't get easier or more forgiving; we get stronger and more resilient." - Steve Maraboli.

Have you ever wondered how some people seem to handle life's challenges with grace and ease, while others crumble under the weight of adversity? It all comes down to resilience and adaptability. In this section, we will explore how Buddhism can help you cultivate these essential qualities and navigate the ups and downs of life.

Resilience is the ability to bounce back from setbacks, to persevere in the face of challenges, and to maintain a positive outlook even in difficult times. Buddhism offers profound wisdom and practical techniques that can strengthen your resilience. Through the practice of meditation and mindfulness, you can develop the mental and emotional fortitude to weather life's storms.

Imagine a tree standing tall in the midst of a raging storm. The wind may bend its branches, but its roots remain firmly grounded. Similarly, by cultivating mindfulness, you can anchor yourself in the present moment, finding stability and inner strength. The teachings of Buddhism encourage us to embrace impermanence and accept that change is an inherent part of life. By developing a deep understanding of this truth, you can let go of attachments and adapt to new circumstances with greater ease.

One of the fundamental concepts in Buddhism is the idea of interconnectedness. We are all part of an intricate web of relationships, and our actions have ripple effects that extend far beyond ourselves. By recognizing this interconnectedness, we can cultivate compassion and empathy toward others. This shift in perspective not only enhances our resilience but also fosters a sense of community and support.

Practicing mindfulness and meditation can also help you develop a greater sense of self-awareness. By observing your thoughts and emotions without judgment, you gain insight into your habitual patterns and reactions. This self-awareness allows you to respond to challenges more thoughtfully and intentionally, rather than reacting impulsively. As you become more attuned to your inner world, you can cultivate a sense of calm and clarity that serves as a foundation for resilience.

Incorporating mindfulness and meditation into your daily life is like building a muscle. It requires consistency and effort, but the rewards are immense. As you navigate the ups and downs of life with greater resilience and adaptability, you will find that challenges become opportunities for growth and transformation. The wisdom of Buddhism provides a roadmap for cultivating these qualities and embracing life's ever-changing nature.

Here's a little exercise for you to try:

- Take a moment to reflect on a recent challenge or setback you faced.

- How did you respond to it?

- Were you able to maintain a sense of resilience and adaptability, or did you feel overwhelmed?

- What lessons can you learn from that experience, and how can you apply Buddhist principles to cultivate greater resilience in the future?

- Write down your reflections and insights in a journal or notebook dedicated to your personal growth journey.

Remember, resilience is not about avoiding difficulties or pretending that everything is perfect. It's about developing the inner resources to navigate life's challenges with grace and strength. By integrating the teachings of Buddhism into your daily life, you can cultivate resilience and adaptability, leading to a more balanced and fulfilling existence.

Chapter Fifteen

CONCLUSION

We've examined the heart of Buddhism, explored its principles, and discovered how its teachings can bring tranquility and balance into our lives. I hope you've found this journey as enlightening and transformative as I have.

Remember when we first started? You were curious, perhaps a little skeptical, about Buddhism and its relevance to your life. You may have been feeling like a hamster on a wheel, constantly running but never really getting anywhere. I hope that by now, you've found some answers, some solace, and perhaps even a new perspective on life.

The beauty of Buddhism lies in its simplicity and its profound wisdom. It teaches us to view matters from a different perspective, to cultivate understanding, loving-kindness, and compassion for ourselves and others. It reminds us to stay in the present, to embrace stillness and silence, and to find calm and peace within ourselves.

The healing that comes from regular practice of mindfulness and meditation is not just spiritual, but physical too. It's like a soothing balm for the soul, a tonic for the body. And the best part? You don't need to be a Buddhist to reap these benefits. Mindfulness and meditation can be practiced separately from any conscious practice of Buddhism. However, an awareness of

Buddhist principles can certainly enhance your life goals and health benefits.

How can a millennia-old philosophy shape and color one's contemporary life? By delving into the pages of this book, I hope you have come to appreciate the profound wisdom encapsulated in the teachings of Buddhism. The very essence of this book, the one in your hands, was born out of my personal journey into the heart of Buddhism.

We began by exploring Buddhism from a bird's eye view, diving into its definitions, origins, beliefs, and its contrasts with other religions. By realizing the inevitability of suffering and its roots in desire, we began to understand the Four Noble Truths, the philosophical bedrock of Buddhism. Through the Eightfold Path, we found a roadmap to free ourselves from the shackles of suffering.

From the Three Jewels to the Five Precepts, the teachings showed us how to cultivate a moral life rooted in compassion and mindfulness. They warned us of the Five Hindrances, the roadblocks to spiritual progress, and taught us the practice of the Four Immeasurables to nourish our hearts with kindness, compassion, joy, and equanimity.

We delved into the sacred silence of meditation and mindfulness, immersing ourselves in the rhythm of our breath and the stillness of our minds. We wrestled with the intricate threads of Karma and Rebirth, weaving a tapestry of understanding about the continuity of existence.

In traversing through the diverse schools of Buddhism, we discovered the flexibility and richness of this ancient tradition. We learned to maintain balance in life, to care for our environment, and to integrate these timeless teachings into the complexity of modern existence.

As I look back, I can see how walking this path has not only transformed my life but also my art. The canvas of my life is now filled with brighter colors and subtler hues. The teachings of Buddhism are not just intellectual knowledge to be studied but wisdom to be lived, like sunlight to be absorbed, not analyzed.

In the final chapter of our journey, we looked towards the path of personal growth and transformation, exploring the crucial role of self-awareness, embracing change, and cultivating resilience. Every step taken in mindfulness, every breath drawn in awareness, every act done with compassion becomes a testament to our commitment to personal growth.

Your Task List:

1. Find a quiet moment to reflect on the lessons learned from each chapter.

2. Jot down three ways you can incorporate these teachings into your daily life.

3. Each day for the next week, meditate for at least 10 minutes, focusing on your breath.

4. Practice one of the Four Immeasurables each week, noting any changes in your mood or perspective.

5. Keep a journal of your journey, documenting your insights and challenges as you navigate the path of Buddhism.

Before we part, let me leave you with this. Life is as beautiful and as complex as a tapestry, woven with threads of joy, sorrow, love, and pain. We all have the power to choose the colors of our threads. So why not choose colors that reflect compassion, peace, love, and understanding? As you close this book, remember, your journey is just beginning. I'd like to leave you with a thought. Life is a journey, not a destination. And every journey is unique, filled with its own challenges and rewards. So, as you continue on your path, remember to be kind to yourself, to others, and to the world around you.

My wish for you is that the teachings of Buddhism serve as a lantern in the darkest nights and a compass in the wildest storms. As you walk this path, may you find serenity in your heart and peace in your mind, one mindful step at a time.

May your path be filled with light.

GLOSSARY

Anatta:
(Non-self) An integral Buddhism idea that negates the concept of an enduring, intrinsic self.

Anicca:
(Impermanence) A core Buddhist principle, advocating the transient and shifting nature of all conditioned phenomena.

Anapanasati:
A form of meditation in Buddhism focusing on mindful breathing.

Bardo Thodol:
(The Tibetan Book of the Dead) A critical Tibetan Buddhist scripture that offers counsel for the journey post-death, elucidating the idea of rebirth.

Bardos:
Stages of existence in the Tibetan tradition, including the stages after death before rebirth.

Brahma Viharas:
(Four Immeasurables) The four supreme states of mind that followers of Buddhism strive to foster: metta (loving-kindness), karuna (compassion), mudita (sympathetic joy), and uppekha (equanimity).

Catur Aryasatyani:
(Four Noble Truths) The bedrock of Buddhist teachings, addressing suffering (Dukkha), its origin, its cessation, and the path leading to its cessation.

Catur Maha Vipassana:
(Four Sights) The four visions that led Siddhartha Gautama on his enlightenment journey: old age, illness, death, and a monk.

Chanda:
(Desire) In Buddhism, a term denoting ethically positive or wholesome desires, distinct from "tanha", which symbolizes craving and is a root of suffering.

Chatvari Magga:
(Eightfold Path) A foundational doctrine in Buddhism, illustrating the path to liberation from suffering (Dukkha).

Dharma / Dhamma:
The teachings of the Buddha, the path of practice and realization.

Dharmachakra:
The Wheel of Dharma, represents the Buddha's teaching of the path to enlightenment.

Dharmata:
The ultimate nature of all things in Buddhism.

Dukkha:
(Suffering) A pivotal concept in Buddhism, often translated as "suffering", but also covers dissatisfaction, unease, and life's intrinsic unsatisfactoriness.

Japa:
A spiritual discipline involving the repetition of a mantra or divine name.

Karuna:
(Compassion) One of the Brahma Viharas (Four Immeasurables) in Buddhism, symbolizes the desire to alleviate all sentient beings' suffering.

Mahayana:
One of the main branches of Buddhism, emphasizes the pursuit of the bodhisattva path.

Magga:
(Path to Cessation of Suffering) Also called the Noble Eightfold Path, it constitutes the fourth of the Four Noble Truths.

Metta:
(Loving Kindness) One of the Brahma Viharas (Four Immeasurables) in Buddhism, reflects unconditional love for all beings without discrimination.

Mudita:
(Sympathetic Joy) One of the Brahma Viharas (Four Immeasurables) in Buddhism, refers to the joy arising from others' happiness.

Nirodha:
(Cessation of Suffering) One of the Four Noble Truths, indicates the potential cessation of suffering.

Nirvana:
The ultimate objective in Buddhism, is a state of liberation and freedom from suffering (Dukkha).

Prajna:
(Wisdom) The comprehension or insight into the true nature of all things, viewed as an essential component of the path to enlightenment in Buddhism.

Pranayama:
A yogic discipline focused on breath control.

Pratityasamutpada:
(Dependant Origination) The Buddhist doctrine of interdependent co-arising, explaining the cycle of birth, suffering, death, and rebirth.

Samadhi:
A state of intense concentration achieved through meditation.

Samatha:
A Buddhist practice of calming the mind and its formations.

Samudaya:
(Origination of Suffering) One of the Four Noble Truths, often associated with desire or craving (tanha).

Samsara:
The cycle of birth, death, and rebirth in Buddhism, from which liberation is desired.

Sampajanna:
Clear comprehension, and awareness of the purpose and suitability of an action.

Sati Sampajanna:
Mindfulness along with clear comprehension, often practiced in Buddhism.

Satipatthana:
The Four Foundations of Mindfulness in Buddhism, consisting of mindfulness of the body, feelings, mind, and phenomena.

Sangha:
The community of Buddhists, one of the Three Jewels of Buddhism.

Sila:
Ethical conduct or morality, one of the components of the Noble Eightfold Path in Buddhism.

Tanha:
Craving or desire, often considered a cause of suffering in Buddhism.

Thangka:
Tibetan Buddhist painting on cotton or silk, often depicting a Buddhist deity, scene, or mandala.

Theravada:
One of the main branches of Buddhism, focuses on the teachings of the earliest texts of Buddhism.

Triratna:
(The Three Jewels) The three pivotal concepts in Buddhism: the Buddha (the enlightened one), the Dharma (the teachings of the Buddha), and the Sangha (the community of Buddhists).

Uppekha:
(Equanimity) One of the Brahma Viharas (Four Immeasurables) in Buddhism, represents a tranquil and balanced mental state regardless of circumstances.

Vajrayana:
A branch of Buddhism often considered part of Mahayana, which uses various ritual practices to achieve enlightenment.

Vipassana:
A Buddhist practice of insight into the true nature of reality.

REFERENCES

Armstrong, K. (2001). Buddha. Penguin Books.

Batchelor, S. (1997). Buddhism without Beliefs: A Contemporary Guide to Awakening. Riverhead Books.

Bodhi, B. (1994). The Noble Eightfold Path: Way to the End of Suffering. Buddhist Publication Society.

Chödrön, P. (1997). The Places That Scare You: A Guide to Fearlessness in Difficult Times. Shambhala Publications.

Dalai Lama. (1995). The World of Tibetan Buddhism: An Overview of Its Philosophy and Practice. Wisdom Publications.

Epstein, M. (1995). Thoughts Without a Thinker: Psychotherapy from a Buddhist Perspective. Basic Books.

Goldstein, J. (2013). Mindfulness: A Practical Guide to Awakening. Sounds True.

Hanh, T. N. (1992). Peace Is Every Step: The Path of Mindfulness in Everyday Life. Bantam Books.

Hanh, T. N. (1998). The Heart of the Buddha's Teaching: Transforming Suffering into Peace, Joy, and Liberation. Broadway Books.

Kabat-Zinn, J. (1994). Wherever You Go, There You Are: Mindfulness Meditation in Everyday Life. Hyperion.

Lopez Jr., D. S. (2001). The Story of Buddhism: A Concise Guide to Its History & Teachings. HarperOne.

"Principles of Buddhist Philosophy in Practice". (2022). Buddhanet.

Rahula, W. (1974). What the Buddha Taught. Grove Press.

Smith, H. (1991). The World's Religions: Our Great Wisdom Traditions. HarperOne.

Trungpa, C. (2002). Cutting Through Spiritual Materialism. Shambhala Publications.

AUTHOR'S NOTE

I wrote this book to share my perspective on the life-affirming and transformational potential of the philosophies of Buddhism, in a way that many books do not cover. Buddhism is an accessible and surprisingly modern philosophy, which may well account for the growth in popularity of Buddhism in the Western world. It fills that desire for many to find a meaningful way to live that is not mired in dogma and directly relates to their own life.

By highlighting the fundamental concepts and principles which the philosophy of Buddhism presents, this book is an accessible way for the reader to change the way they see the world, by understanding that how they view themselves and how they behave is at the very heart of everything. This realization, and integrating the precepts into their lives, leads to self-understanding. The definition of self-understanding is *"the key to the successful resolution of any emotional problem"*, which is something many of us strive for in our lives.

Compassion, empathy, and wisdom are qualities of emotional intelligence which evolve through the active practice of Buddhist philosophies.

If you've enjoyed this book, I would greatly appreciate your support in leaving it a review. I read every review, and your valuable feedback not only provides insights into your thoughts after reading this book but also helps me improve.

It also does wonders in helping others discover this book.

Please follow links below:

US – https://amazon.com/dp/9798856220697

UK – https://amazon.co.uk/dp/9798856220697

Thank you.

About The Author

Rohini Heendeniya was born in Sri Lanka and comes from a family who have been practicing Buddhists for generations. She grew up in the UK from the age of 6. She had a varied career: in television, public relations, transport, and property, and gained a business management degree in her early 40s. She worked in senior management roles but eventually found a career in the corporate world unsatisfying and lacking in spiritual meaning. She trained as a therapist and life coach, in a range of energy meridian therapies, energetic healing modalities, past life regression therapy, and many other techniques. She has had a lifelong interest in exploring the nature of the human experience, and a deep spiritual belief that has enhanced that exploration. She subsequently began a career as a writer. She lives on the south coast of England.

Also By This Author

The Essential Beginner's Guide to
Meditation and Mindfulness

SPIRITUAL PRACTICE Series
Publishing in August 2023
Tarot Reference Guide, Workbook, and Journal
by Maya Quinn

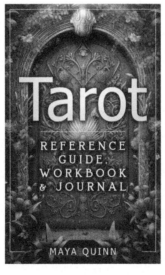

Made in the USA
Las Vegas, NV
31 August 2023

76914178R00075